3

CHILDREN'S ISSUES, LAWS AND PROGRAMS

CHILD WELFARE: FEDERAL ROLE IN ASSISTANCE AND IMPROVEMENT

CHILDREN'S ISSUES, LAWS AND PROGRAMS

Additional books in this series can be found on Nova's website under the Series tab.

Additional E-books in this series can be found on Nova's website under the E-books tab.

CHILDREN'S ISSUES, LAWS AND PROGRAMS

CHILD WELFARE: FEDERAL ROLE IN ASSISTANCE AND IMPROVEMENT

MIGUEL G. RAPOSO
AND
DANIELLE M. CARROCA
EDITORS

Nova Science Publishers, Inc.
New York

For permission to use material from this book please contact us:
Telephone 631-231-7269; Fax 631-231-8175
Web Site: http://www.novapublishers.com

NOTICE TO THE READER

Additional color graphics may be available in the e-book version of this book.

LIBRARY OF CONGRESS CATALOGING-IN-PUBLICATION DATA
Child welfare : federal role in assistance and improvement / editors, Miguel G. Raposo and Danielle M. Carroca.
p. cm.
Includes index.
ISBN 978-1-61209-704-6 (softcover)
1. Children--Legal status, laws, etc.--United States. 2. Federal aid to child welfare--United States. 3. United States. Fostering Connections to Success and Increasing Adoptions Act of 2008. I. Raposo, Miguel G. II. Carroca, Danielle M.
KF3731.A56C48 2011
344.7303'27--dc22

2011011536

Published by Nova Science Publishers, Inc. † New York

CONTENTS

PREFACE

Child welfare services are intended to prevent the abuse or neglect of children and to ensure that children have safe, permanent homes, in addition to promoting the well-being of children and their families. Most federal child welfare programs are administered by the Administration for Children and Families (ACF) within the U.S. Department of Health and Human Services (HHS). This new book provides an overview of the federal role in the assistance and improvement of child welfare services. Discussed in this compilation are The Fostering Connections to Success and Increasing Adoptions Act of 2008; Social Security and Supplemental Security Income (SSI) benefits for children in foster care; and the most recent and proposed federal funding for child welfare programs.

Chapter 1- The Fostering Connections to Success and Increasing Adoptions Act of 2008 (H.R. 6893) is an omnibus child welfare bill designed to ensure greater permanence and improve the well-being of children served by public child welfare agencies. The legislation received strong support in Congress and, beyond revising and extending the Adoption Incentives program, responds to a range of issues and concerns that have been raised (some for more than a decade) by public child welfare administrators; youth, adoption, tribal, and child welfare advocates; and by children and youth who have been (or still are) in foster care. The bill passed the House of Representatives, by voice vote (under suspension of the rules), on September 17, 2008, and the Senate, by unanimous consent, on September 22, 2008. It was signed into law by the President on October 7, 2008 (P.L. 110-351).

Chapter 2- An estimated 30,000 children receive Supplemental Security Income (S SI) or other Social Security benefits while in foster care. SSI benefits are available under Title XVI of the Social Security Act for certain disabled children from families with low incomes and minimal assets. Social Security benefits may be paid under Title II of the act to the children of workers who have retired, become disabled, or died.

Chapter 3- Child welfare services and supports are intended to ensure and improve the safety, permanence, and well-being of children. The President's FY2011 budget seeks close to $8.5 12 billion for the child welfare programs discussed in this report. This request is $80 million above the FY2010 funding appropriated for those programs as part of the Consolidated Appropriations Act, 2010 (P.L. 111-117). Congress has not yet finalized FY2011 appropriations. However, on September 30, 2010, President Obama signed the Continuing Appropriations Act, 2011 (P.L. 111-242). That law generally extends federal funding, at the levels provided in FY20 10, until December 3, 2010, or until full-year funding is enacted, whichever happens first. For child welfare programs, the Senate Appropriations Committee has recommended full-year FY20 11 funding at a level similar to the President's request. Most child welfare programs are administered by the Administration for Children and Families (ACF) within the Department of Health and Human Services (HHS). However, a few are administered by the Office of Justice Programs at the Department of Justice.

In: Child Welfare: Federal Role in Assistance... ISBN: 978-1-61209-704-6
Editors: M.G. Raposo, D.M. Carroca

Chapter 1

CHILD WELFARE: THE FOSTERING CONNECTIONS TO SUCCESS AND INCREASING ADOPTIONS ACT OF 2008

Emilie Stoltzfus

SUMMARY

The Fostering Connections to Success and Increasing Adoptions Act of 2008 (H.R. 6893) is an omnibus child welfare bill designed to ensure greater permanence and improve the well-being of children served by public child welfare agencies. The legislation received strong support in Congress and, beyond revising and extending the Adoption Incentives program, responds to a range of issues and concerns that have been raised (some for more than a decade) by public child welfare administrators; youth, adoption, tribal, and child welfare advocates; and by children and youth who have been (or still are) in foster care. The bill passed the House of Representatives, by voice vote (under suspension of the rules), on September 17, 2008, and the Senate, by unanimous consent, on September 22, 2008. It was signed into law by the President on October 7, 2008 (P.L. 110-351).

The final bill represented a compromise between earlier bills acted on in the House (H.R. 6307) and in the Senate Finance Committee (S. 3038). As enacted, it revises the Adoption Incentives program and extends its funding authorization for five years (FY2009-FY2013). It makes significant changes to federal funding for child welfare programs, which include authorizing new federal support for states that provide kinship guardianship assistance to eligible children leaving foster care; expanding eligibility for federal adoption assistance (by phasing out, over FY2010- FY2018, income and other eligibility criteria that are based on dated cash welfare program rules); extending, as of FY2011, eligibility for federal foster care assistance to youth who remain in care beyond their 18th birthday, up to age 21; and phasing in additional support to states for child welfare related training. Additionally, the bill authorizes tribal child welfare agencies, as of FY20 10, to directly access federal funds for foster care, adoption, and guardianship assistance under the Title IV-E program, provided the tribes meet substantially the same requirements made of states. The bill also appropriates $15 million in annual funding, for five years, for a new competitive grant program, Family Connection Grants.

Apart from these financing changes, P.L. 110-351 establishes new requirements for receipt of federal child welfare funding by public child welfare agencies. These include several that focus exclusively on the health and education status of children in foster care and others intended to ensure, or enable, sibling and other kinship connections for children in, or entering, foster care, and those leaving to adoption or guardianship. The bill also requires states to make new efforts related to planning for the transition of older children leaving foster care for independent living and requires states to inform prospective adoptive parents of foster children of their potential eligibility for the adoption tax credit (under the federal tax code).

Many of the changes included in the new law are projected by the Congressional Budget Office (CBO) to increase federal spending for child welfare. However, the increases are projected to be fully offset (over the next five and ten years) by savings or increased revenues to the federal treasury that CBO expects to be produced by other changes in the bill (both related and unrelated to child welfare policy). This report may be updated if warranted by issues related to implementing the new law.

The Fostering Connections to Success and Increasing Adoptions Act of 2008 (H.R. 6893) is an omnibus child welfare bill designed to ensure greater permanence and improve the well-being of children served by public child welfare agencies — especially children in foster care, those who leave foster care in their later teens, and those who are Indian children. The legislation received strong support in Congress, and beyond revising and extending the Adoption Incentives program, it responds to a range of issues and concerns that have been variously raised (some for more than a decade) by public child welfare administrators; youth, adoption, tribal, and child welfare advocates; and by children and youth who have been (or still are) in foster care. The bill passed the House of Representatives, by voice vote (under suspension of the rules), on September 17 and the Senate, by unanimous consent, on September 22, 2008. It was signed into law by President George W. Bush on October 7, 2008. P.L. 110-351 represents a compromise between provisions that were included in the Improved Adoption Incentives and Relative Guardianship Support Act of 2008 (S. 3038, introduced by Senator Charles Grassley), as approved by the Senate Finance Committee on September 10, 2008 (S.Rept. 110-467), and the Fostering Connections to Success Act (H.R. 6307, introduced by Representative Jim McDermott with Representative Jerry Weller), as passed by the House on June 24, 2008.[1]

Overview of the Bill

The Fostering Connections to Success and Increasing Adoptions Act of 2008 (P.L. 110-351) revises and extends the Adoption Incentives program (under Section 473A of the Social Security Act) for five years, authorizes states to claim additional federal funds for certain child welfare purposes and adds new requirements for receipt of federal child welfare dollars. These changes are primarily designed to better ensure the well-being of children in foster care, to increase support for permanent living arrangements outside of foster care, to better support the transition of older foster youth to independent living, and to enable tribes to directly access federal support for foster care, kinship care, and adoption assistance provided to Indian children under their authority.

Financing Changes. P.L. 110-351 enacts the broadest changes to federal financial support for child welfare programs under Title IV-E of the Social Security Act, since that part of the law was created by the Adoption Assistance and Child Welfare Act of 1980 (P.L. 96-272). Among those changes, the bill

- permits states to claim open-ended federal reimbursement for a part of all eligible state costs related to providing kinship guardianship assistance;

- permits states to claim open-ended federal reimbursement for a part of the cost of making maintenance payments on behalf of eligible children who are in foster care beyond their 18th birthday (until their 21st birthday), provided those youths are in school, working, or engaged in a related activity (effective with FY2011);
- authorizes direct access for tribes to open-ended federal reimbursement for the costs of operating a foster care, adoption assistance, and kinship guardianship assistance program on behalf of children under tribal authority, provided those tribes meet substantially the same requirements made of states receiving these funds (effective with FY2010);
- expands federal support for adoption assistance by de-linking, over time (FY2010-FY2018), eligibility for that program from income and other criteria that were a part of the prior law cash welfare program, Aid to Families with Dependent Children (AFDC); and
- phases-in (FY2009-FY2013) authorization for states to claim open-ended federal reimbursement for a larger share of their short-term training costs for staff of state licensed or approved (private) child welfare agencies and to receive reimbursement, at this same increased rate, for eligible short-term training costs of current or prospective relative guardians and certain court or court-related personnel who handle child abuse and neglect cases.

In addition, P.L. 110-351 provides $15 million annually (FY2009-FY2013) for Family Connection Grants to support kinship navigator programs, family group decision making meetings, intensive family-finding efforts, and residential treatment centers for families (under Title IV-B of the Social Security Act). And it appropriates $3 million annually (FY2009 and every succeeding fiscal year) for technical assistance and implementation grants related to improving outcomes for Indian children (under Title IV-E).

New Requirements. Apart from expanding child welfare funding options for states, P.L. 110-351 establishes new requirements for receipt of federal child welfare funding by public child welfare agencies. The bill requires these agencies (under Title IV-E or Title IV-B) to

- provide assurance that each school-age child receiving federal foster care, adoption, or guardianship assistance is enrolled in school;

- work with other appropriate public agencies to reduce unnecessary school moves for all children in foster care and, separately, to coordinate and ensure access to health care for them, including mental health services and dental care;
- make "reasonable efforts" to place siblings together, whether in foster care, adoption, or guardianship;
- notify the adult relatives of children entering foster care of their options to participate in the care and placement of the child;
- no more than 90 days before a youth's exit from the foster care system (due to age rather than placement with a permanent family) develop with the youth a specific plan for his or her transition to independent living;
- negotiate "in good faith" with a tribe in the state that requests an agreement with the state to receive federal (Title IV-E) funds in return for that tribe's administration of some or all of the Title IV-E foster care, adoption assistance, and kinship guardianship assistance program for Indian children under its authority; and
- inform prospective adoptive parents of foster children of their potential eligibility for the federal adoption tax credit.

P.L. 110-351 makes additional child welfare financing, policy, or related program changes, which are detailed below. Finally, and unrelated to child welfare policy, it amends the federal tax code's uniform definition of child (for purposes of claiming a variety of credits or deductions) and it makes changes to certain investment rules for the Treasury Department. Those specific policy changes, together with savings projected from the implementation of guardianship assistance and the school enrollment requirement, are estimated by the Congressional Budget Office (CBO) to fully offset the federal cost of the increased spending authorized by the bill over the next 5 to 10 years. All of the child welfare policy changes in P.L. 110-351 are made to programs or parts of the law that are administered by the Administration for Children and Families (ACF), within the U.S. Department of Health and Human Services (HHS), and are expected to be implemented by ACF.[2]

This report begins with a more detailed and topical summary of the provisions of H.R. 6893, as enacted, including some legislative background and context. It continues by reviewing the cost estimates for the provisions, as projected by CBO, and then discusses the legislative origins of the enacted bill and Administration views of provisions included in related predecessor bills

(H.R. 6307 and S. 3038). It closes with a section-by-section description of the bill's provisions.

New and Expanded Assistance or Activities Related to Permanence

The Fostering Connections to Success and Increasing Adoptions Act of 2008 (P.L. 110-351) makes a number of financing and policy changes that are designed to encourage and support children's placement in a permanent family — whether through strengthened or re-established connections with biological kin or through federal support and incentives to support children's adoption out of foster care.

Permanence via Family Connections. The enacted bill permits states to claim federal support for kinship guardianship assistance (under Title IV-E of the Social Security Act), makes other policy changes expected to promote or facilitate relative placement, authorizes and provides funding for Family Connection Grants, and requires states to make reasonable efforts to place siblings together.

Kinship Guardianship Assistance. The enacted bill permits states to claim open-ended reimbursement under Title IV-E for kinship guardianship assistance provided on behalf of eligible children who leave foster care for placement in a legal guardianship with a relative. As amended by the Adoption and Safe Families Act of 1997 (ASFA, P.L. 105-89), federal statute defines "legal guardianship" (for purposes of Title IV-E and Title IV-B of the Social Security Act) as "a judicially created relationship between child and caretaker which is intended to be permanent and self- sustaining as evidenced by the transfer to the caretaker of the following parental rights with respect to the child: protection, education, care and control of the person, custody of the person, and decisionmaking."[3] States are entitled to claim federal reimbursement for the cost of providing kinship guardianship assistance payments on behalf of eligible children at their Federal Medical Assistance Percentage (FMAP), which may range from a low of 50%, in states with higher per capita income, to 83%, in those with lower per capita income. States opting to provide such payments may also claim reimbursement of eligible general administrative costs at a 50% federal reimbursement rate, and for program-related training costs at 75% federal reimbursement, (although some of these eligible training costs will initially be reimbursed at a lower rate; see "Federal Support for Training and Other Changes" below).

Since the middle 1 990s, close to 40 states have implemented some kind of subsidized guardianship program for children leaving foster care. However, many of those programs were not statewide and not all have been maintained.[4] Under child welfare "waivers," as many as 11 of those states have experimented with subsidized guardianship programs using federal Title IV-E funds.[5] Some of those earliest experiments found that providing guardianship subsidies increased exits to permanence for children in foster care and that on a range of safety and well-being measures, children placed in subsidized guardianship settings fared at least as well as did children placed in other permanent settings.[6]

In May 2004, the Pew Commission on Children in Foster Care recommended federal support of subsidized guardianship (under Title IV-E of the Social Security Act) as part of a broader package of child welfare financing reform measures. In July 2007, citing evidence that the subsidies "could help states increase the number of permanent homes available to African American and other children in foster care," the Government Accountability Office (GAO) recommended that Congress consider authorizing federal subsidies for legal guardianship.[7] In its report approving guardianship assistance provisions similar to those that became a part of the final legislation, the Senate Finance Committee cited both the child welfare waivers and academic research to assert that children in kinship placements, including relative guardianships, have improved well-being; that guardianship is a good permanency option for children in foster care; and that provision of a state option to receive federal support for guardianship assistance under Title IV-E is expected to reduce federal costs under Title IV-E (by reducing the need for federal reimbursement of case planning and case review activities on behalf of children moved permanently from foster care to guardianship).[8]

Changes to Promote or Facilitate Relative Placement. The option to use federal Title IV-E funds to support children in kinship guardianship is only one of a number of changes included in P.L. 110-351 that seek to strengthen children's connections to their families and to create more opportunity for kinship placements (whether guardianship or otherwise).[9] These include

- a new plan requirement (under Title IV-E) that states "exercise due diligence" to identify grandparents and other adult relatives of a child, within 30 days of removing the child from the custody of his/her parents, and to notify those relatives of the child's removal and the relatives' options for participating in the care and placement of the child, including information about foster family home licensing and, as applicable, guardianship assistance;[10]

- codification of existing guidance (regarding a Title IV-E state plan requirement) that provides that when applying the state's foster family home licensing standards to the home of a relative caregiver, the state may — on a case-by-case basis and for a specific child only — waive any "non-safety"licensing requirement;
- a mandated study and report (by HHS) on the use of licensed and unlicensed relative foster family homes, including information on the frequency and kind of non-safety standards waived by states and recommendations for actions that might increase the number of children in foster care who are safely placed in licensed relative foster family homes; and
- authorization for HHS to make comparisons of names submitted by child welfare agencies to information in the Federal Parent Locator System (FPLS), which may aid in identifying or locating relatives.[11]

Family Connection Grants. Further, the bill establishes a new competitive grant program, under Title IV-B, Subpart 1 of the Social Security Act named Family Connection Grants. Under this program, public child welfare agencies (state, local or tribal), and non-profit private organizations may seek federal funding to help children — whether they are in foster care or at-risk of entering foster care — connect (or reconnect) with birth parents or other extended kin. Specifically, the funds must be used to establish or support one or more of the following:

- **kinship navigator programs,** which through information referral systems and other means, assist kinship caregivers in learning about, finding, and using programs and services to meet their own needs and those of the children they are raising;
- **intensive family-finding efforts** that use search technology to locate biological kin of children and then work to reestablish relationships and to explore permanent family placements for these children;
- **family group decision-making meetings** that enable families to develop plans that nurture children and protect them from abuse and neglect, and, when appropriate, must safely facilitate connecting

children exposed to domestic violence to relevant services and reconnecting them with the abused parent; and
- **residential family treatment** centers that enable parents and children to live together in a safe environment for not less than six months and that provide, onsite or by referral, a full range of services to meet the needs of the family, including substance abuse treatment, early childhood intervention, family counseling, mental health services, medical care, and other services.

HHS is permitted to award up to 30 new Family Connection Grants each year and may not award a grant for a period of less than one year nor more than three years. Grantees are required to provide matching funds equal to no less than 25% of the total approved grant program costs in years one and two of a grant and no less than 50% in year three. The enacted bill appropriates $15 million for the Family Connection Grants in each of FY2009-FY2013, of which $5 million must be used annually to support kinship navigator programs.

Reasonable Efforts to Place Siblings Together. Finally, unless the state documents that doing so would be contrary to the safety or welfare of a sibling, the bill requires states (under the Title IV-E state plan) to make "reasonable efforts" to place siblings together, whether in foster care, kinship guardianship assistance, or adoption. It further stipulates that, whenever a joint placement is not made, the state must make "reasonable efforts" to provide for "frequent visitation or other ongoing interaction" between the siblings, unless the state documents that the facilitated contact is contrary to the safety or well-being of any one of the siblings.

Permanence via Adoption. P.L. 110-351 also expands eligibility for federal adoption assistance to children with special needs, revises and extends the Adoption Incentives program, and requires states to provide information to prospective adoptive parents concerning the adoption tax credit.

Phasing Out Income Eligibility and Related Rules for Adoption Assistance. The enacted bill phases out (FY2010-FY201 8) the use of income tests as part of determining eligibility for federal adoption assistance. This change will provide more federal support to special needs children who leave foster care for adoption. States must continue to pay a part of the cost of providing this support but are required to use any state funds that would be saved because of this expanded federal eligibility for adoption assistance on child welfare purposes.[12]

Federal adoption assistance was established in 1980 (P.L. 96-272) for children determined by their state to have "special needs."[13] The vast majority of these children, then and now, are children adopted out of foster care. The 1980 law also stipulated that to be eligible for federal adoption assistance a child must either be eligible for Supplemental Security Income (SSI) or have been removed from the home of birth parents in which he or she met the income and other eligibility criteria of the federal cash welfare program (Aid to Families with Dependent Children, AFDC).[14] AFDC was repealed in 1996 by the Personal Responsibility and Work Opportunity Reconciliation Act (PRWORA, P.L. 104-193). However, federal eligibility for Title IV-E assistance continues to be linked to AFDC eligibility rules as those rules existed (on July 16, 1996) prior to the program's repeal. Beginning in FY20 10 (and continuing through FY20 18), P.L. 110-351 will phase out this link for adoption assistance, which the Senate Finance Committee describes as "an inappropriate eligibility factor for Federal Adoption Assistance."[15] (As included in the enacted bill, the revised eligibility rules for federal adoption assistance also eliminate any income- or resource-related eligibility requirements that apply to special needs children who have physical or medical disabilities that qualify them for Supplemental Security Income, SSI.).

The revised eligibility rules will become effective in FY2010, but only for children who are age 16 or older when their adoption assistance agreement is finalized. With each new fiscal year, this age will be lowered (by two years) so that by FY2018 any child with special needs may qualify for federal adoption assistance under the revised rules. In addition, beginning in FY2010, any child who has been in foster care for 60 continuous months may qualify for federal adoption assistance under the revised eligibility rules (regardless of age) and any sibling of a child who is eligible under the revised rules (whether due to age or length of stay in care) may also qualify under those criteria. Throughout this eight-year phase-in period, the eligibility criteria that applied prior to the passage of H.R. 6893, including the link to AFDC eligibility, will continue to apply to any child who does not qualify for eligibility determination under the revised rules (at the time his or her adoption assistance agreement is finalized).

Reauthorization of the Adoption Incentives Program. Apart from the expanded support for federal adoption assistance, the Fostering Connections to Success and Increasing Adoptions Act of 2008 continues incentives to states for increased adoptions from foster care by revising and extending the

Adoption Incentives program. This program was created by ASFA (P.L. 105-89) and was initially extended in 2003 by P.L. 108-145. A state earns a bonus for each eligible adoption out of foster care that is above its baseline number of adoptions. States earn an award for increases in total adoptions, increases in adoption of older children (age 9 and above) and, they may also receive an award for increases in the number of adoptions of children with special needs who are under the age of 9. For adoptions finalized in FY2007 (most recent year for which awards were made), 21 states earned a total of $1 1.1 million in bonus funds.[16] States are permitted to spend this award money to provide any service to children or families, including post-adoption services, that is authorized by the major federal child welfare programs (under Title IV-B or Title IV-E of the Social Security Act).

P.L. 110-351 continues, through FY2013, the current annual funding authorization of $43 million for the Adoption Incentive program. It doubles the incentive amounts states may earn for each increase in the number of older children adopted from foster care (from $4,000 to $8,000) and for children with special needs, under age 9, who are adopted from foster care (from $2,000 to $4,000). The incentive award for any increase in the total number of children adopted from foster care was not changed and remains at $4,000. The enacted bill also makes other changes to the incentive structure of the program, which are intended to ensure that states (even those with declining overall foster care caseloads) continue to have a fiscal incentive to increase adoptions. These changes include fixing each state's baseline adoption numbers at the numbers achieved in FY2007 and allowing (provided sufficient appropriations) a new incentive payment for states that increase the rate of children adopted from foster care.[17] To earn an award for an increased rate of adoptions, the state must increase the share of children adopted out of its foster care caseload (that is its foster child adoption rate) above the highest such rate it previously achieved, in any year, beginning with FY2002 and ending with the year just prior to the award year. The amount of the award is $1,000 times the increased number of adoptions achieved by the state that are attributed to the increased adoption rate.[18] The increased incentive payment amounts and the incentives for states increasin g the rate at which children are adopted out of their foster care caseload, will be used to calculate awards earned by states for adoptions finalized in FY2008. Those awards are expected to be announced in September 2009. Finally, P.L. 110-351 also ensures that states have a full 24 months to spend any adoption incentive funding awarded.

Information on Adoption Tax Credit. As part of supporting the goal of increasing permanence for foster children through adoption, P.L. 110-351 requires states (under Title IV-E), to provide notice to any individual who is adopting a child out of foster care (or who the state learns is considering such an adoption) of the individual's potential eligibility for the federal adoption tax credit. The credit is adjusted annually for inflation and for tax year 2008 equals $11,650 for individuals who adopt children with "special needs."[19]

Support for Older Foster Youth and Transition to Independent Living

The Fostering Connections to Success and Improving Adoptions Act of 2008 (P.L. 110-351) also seeks to strengthen support for children whose permanency outcome is "independent living." These are youth who "emancipate" from foster care; that is, they are released from state foster care custody because they have reached the state age of majority (typically age 18) rather than because they have been placed with a permanent family. At least since the middle 1 980s (P.L. 99-272), Congress has sought to better aid the transition of these youth from foster care to independent living. With the Chafee Foster Care Independence Act of 1999 (P.L. 106-169), Congress significantly expanded support for services to youth both before and after they "age-out" and in 2001 (P.L. 107-133), it authorized funds for Education and Training Vouchers for these youth. Even so the number of children leaving foster care via emancipation continues to grow — reaching close to 27,000 youth in FY2006 — and, in general, their school, work, and other important life outcomes continue to be poor.[20]

Option to Extend Support for Youth Remaining in Care to Age 21. P.L. 110-351 takes a new tack in responding to this longstanding concern by permitting states, as of FY20 11, to provide continued federal foster care maintenance payments on behalf of eligible children even after they have reached their 1 8th birthday. Under current law, federal Title IV-E assistance ends with a child's 1 8th birthday, (or, possibly, the 19th if the child is still completing high school). Specifically, the enacted bill permits states to continue to seek open-ended federal reimbursement for a part of the cost of providing maintenance payments to eligible children who remain in foster care after their 18th birthday, provided those children have not yet reached their 21st birthday and are either enrolled in school, employed at least 80 hours a month, or participating in an activity designed to promote or remove barriers to employment. States may exempt a youth from these requirements so long as the youth has a medical condition making him or her incapable of participating in the activity, and this incapacity is supported by regularly updated information in his or her case plan. P.L. 110-351 also permits continued support to youth in foster care (age 18 or older) who are living independently in a supervised setting and it stipulates that HHS must define, in regulation, what qualifies as such a setting.[21]

New Transition Planning Requirement. Separately, the bill requires each state (as part of its mandatory case review system) to have a procedure that ensures every child leaving foster care has a transition plan created on his or her behalf. The transition plan must be created with the youth by a caseworker and, as appropriate, other representative(s) of the child — no earlier than 90 days before the child's 18th birthday (or at whatever later age chosen by the state to end foster care assistance). It must address specific options for the youth with regard to housing, health insurance, education, local opportunities for mentors and continuing support services, as well as workforce supports and employment services.

Option to Extend Support for Youth Leaving Care for Permanent Home After Reaching Age 16. With limited exceptions, monthly federal (Title IV-E) assistance has not generally been available for a child who has reached his or her 18th birthday and who left foster care for a permanent family via adoption or kinship guardianship. However, P.L. 110-351 permits states, as of FY2011, to choose to continue federally supported subsidies on behalf of eligible children who leave foster care *after* their 16th birthday for adoption or kinship guardianship so long as those youth have not yet reached their *21st birthday*, and are enrolled in school, employed at least 80 hours a month, or participating in an activity designed to promote or remove barriers to employment. (States may exempt a child from these school, work or other engagement requirements if the child has a medical condition that makes him or her incapable of participating in the activity, and this incapacity is supported by regularly updated information in the child's case plan.) In addition, a state is allowed to continue federal adoption assistance or *kinship guardianship* assistance up to the 21st birthday on behalf of any child, regardless of the age at which the child left foster care, if the state determines that "the child has a mental or physical handicap that warrants the continuation of assistance." (This was and remains true with regard to adoption assistance;

P.L. 110-351 will also extend it, as of FY201 1, to kinship guardianship assistance.)

Services For Youth Leaving Foster Care After Reaching Age 16. Finally, the enacted bill expands the purposes of the Chafee Foster Care Independence Program to provide that any of the activities or services provided in support of independent living for youth who are expected to age out of foster care without a permanent family, may also be provided to youth who leave foster care at age 16 or older, to either adoption or guardianship. The bill also extends eligibility for Education and Training Vouchers (which are valued at $5,000 annually and may be used for the cost of attending college or an equivalent training program) to youth who leave foster care for guardianship after their 16th birthday. (Children who leave foster care for adoption after their 16th birthday continue to be eligible for these vouchers as was true under prior law.)

Well-Being of Children in Foster Care

The Fostering Connections to Success and Increasing Adoptions Act of 2008 (P.L. 110-351) makes new requirements of states that focus on ensuring and enabling stable enrollment in school for children in foster care and on their access to needed and appropriate health care, including mental health services and dental care. For more then a decade, the primary goals of federal child welfare policy have commonly been expressed as achieving safety, permanency, and well-being for children. However, the health- and education-related requirements included in P.L. 110-351 are among the first federal *statutory* requirements of child welfare agencies that focus specifically on the well-being of children in foster care — as distinct from their need for safety and permanence.[22]

Education Stability and Enrollment. Specifically, P.L. 110-351 requires state child welfare agencies — as part of the Title IV-E case plan requirements that apply to each child in foster care — to work with relevant state and local education authorities to ensure that a child remains in the same school in which he or she is enrolled at the time of foster care placement, or, if this is not in the best interests of the child, to ensure immediate and appropriate enrollment for the child in a new school. To help support this requirement, the enacted bill permits states to claim federal funding for the cost of transporting children to their "school of origin" at the same reimbursement rate that is provided for foster care maintenance payments. (That rate ranges from 50%-83%, with states with higher per capita incomes receiving a lower federal reimbursement rate and vice versa.[23]) Separately (under the Title IV-E plan), P.L. 110-351 requires states to assure that children who have reached the minimum age for mandatory school attendance in their state, and who are receiving federal foster care maintenance payments, adoption assistance, or kinship guardianship assistance, are enrolled in school or have completed high school.

Health Care Oversight. Further (under Title IV-B, Subpart 1), the new law requires each state to develop a coordinated strategy and oversight plan to ensure access to health care, including mental health services and dental care, for all children in foster care. This coordinated strategy and oversight plan must be a collaborative effort between the state child welfare agency and the state agency that administers Medicaid (in consultation with pediatric and other health care experts, as well as experts in, or recipients of, child welfare services). Among other things, the strategy and plan must outline: a schedule for initial and follow-up health screens; how the health needs identified by those screens will be monitored and treated; how medical information for children in care will be updated and appropriately shared; steps to ensure continuity of health care services; and oversight of prescription medicines.

These new health- and education-related requirements are unique in federal child welfare policy because they look beyond the safety and permanence needs of children in foster care and focus instead on measures of well-being that are considered relevant to *any* child in the nation.[24] Safety and permanence are also critical to the well-being of all children. However, by definition, they are issues of immediate and special concern for children in foster care. Accordingly, federal child welfare policy has long focused on ways to better achieve and ensure them. Notably, the Adoption Assistance and Child Welfare Act of 1980 (P.L. 9 6-272) recognized the critical need for permanence by providing new incentives for case planning for each child in foster care and by authorizing federal support for adoption assistance to children leaving foster care. Further, more than a decade ago, ASFA (P.L. 105-89) asserted the primacy of safety in all child welfare decisions and reinvigorated attention to permanence for children in foster care by establishing new case planning and case review timetables and requirements, and by establishing the Adoption Incentives program.

Direct Federal Support to Tribal Programs

The Fostering Connections to Success and Increasing Adoptions Act of 2008 (P.L. 110-351) seeks to improve the child welfare services and supports available to Indian children by granting tribes (as of FY2010) the same authority that states have to seek federal reimbursement of a part of all their eligible foster care, adoption, and kinship guardianship assistance costs. Indian children may currently be eligible for Title IV-E assistance if they are in the care and placement responsibility of a state. However, children under the care and placement responsibility of a tribe may not receive this assistance *unless* the tribe's responsibility of the child is "supervised" by the state via a state-tribal cooperative agreement. Explaining their approval of direct tribal access to federal Title IV-E support — which has been a goal of tribal child welfare advocates for many years and has been proposed in every Congress since at least the 105th (1997) — the Senate Finance Committee stated that "tribes, tribal consortia, and tribal organizations may provide higher quality and more culturally appropriate care for Indian children."[25]

To receive Title IV-E funds, a tribe, tribal organization, or tribal consortium[26] must submit a plan for approval to HHS and, with specific and limited exceptions, must meet all the requirements for receipt of this funding "in the same manner" as they are required of states. The bill also permits tribes (as of FY2010) to apply to HHS and receive a direct federal allotment of Chafee Foster Care Independence and/or Education and Training Voucher funds. In addition, it stipulates that current "cooperative agreements" — agreements between a tribe and state, which permit a tribe to receive federal Title IV-E funds via the state — must continue unchanged, unless either party with the right to revoke or change the agreement elects to do so.

P.L. 110-351 provides for calculation of a tribe-specific federal matching rate for foster care maintenance payments, adoption assistance payments, and kinship guardianship assistance payments (a "tribal FMAP"). Tribes with an approved Title IV-E plan are to receive this reimbursement rate directly from the federal government. If a tribe has a cooperative agreement or contract with a state to administer Title IV-E payments, that state is to receive reimbursement at the tribal FMAP for the portion of its Title IV-E foster care maintenance, adoption assistance or kinship guardianship assistance payments that are made under the state-tribal agreement or contract. Further, as of FY2010, P.L. 110-351 requires a state to negotiate "in good faith" with any eligible tribal entity in the state if that tribal entity requests to enter into an agreement with the state under which the state would provide Title IV-E funds to the tribe for it to administer all or part of the program on behalf of children under tribal authority. A state will similarly be required to negotiate in good faith with any tribal entity in the state that is not receiving a direct federal allotment of Chafee Foster Care Independence Program and/or Education and Training Voucher funds and which requests an agreement or contract that would allow it to receive funds from the state to administer the program(s) on behalf of Indian children under its authority.

Finally, to help ensure these new provisions result in improved outcomes for Indian children, the bill appropriates $3 million (for FY2009 and every succeeding year) for technical assistance to tribes and states and for implementation grants to tribes that are preparing to submit a Title IV-E plan for approval to HHS. These implementation grants may be worth as much as $300,000. A tribal entity may receive this grant only once and it must agree to submit a Title IV-E plan to HHS for approval no later than 24 months after receiving the grant funding. If the plan is not submitted within 24 months the tribe must repay the entire grant amount. However, HHS must waive this repayment requirement if the tribe's failure to submit it within 24 months was a result of a "circumstances beyond the control" of the tribe.

Federal Support for Training and Other Changes

Over five years, P.L. 110-351 phases in an increased federal reimbursement rate for states that offer short-term training to workers at private, licensed child welfare agencies — provided this training is related to the Title IV-E foster care, adoption, and kinship guardianship program. The enacted bill also permit states to claim Title IV-E training reimbursement for certain short-term training of current and prospective relative guardians and for court and related personnel (including attorneys) who handle child abuse and neglect cases. The bill sets the federal matching rate for costs of providing short-term training to private agency workers, current and prospective relative guardians, and for certain court or court-related personnel handling abuse and neglect cases at 55% in FY2009, rising 5% annually until it reaches 75% in FY2013. (Title IV-E training costs that were reimbursed at 75% before passage of H.R. 6893 will continue to be reimbursed at that same level throughout this phase-in period.)

P.L. 110-351 makes several changes that are unrelated to child welfare policy. These include clarifying the uniform definition of child that is used for a variety of federal tax code purposes. It also amends the law to permit the

Treasury Department to invest excess operating cash for 90 days in repurchase agreements. These non- child welfare-related provisions — together with savings projected from the implementation of kinship guardianship assistance and the school enrollment requirement — are estimated by the Congressional Budget Office (CBO) to fully offset the cost of the bill to the federal treasury over the next five and 10 years.

Finally, the bill prohibits any interpretation of its provisions that would "alter" any current "prohibitions on Federal payments to individuals who are unlawfully present in the United States."

Effective Date

Unless otherwise stipulated, the provisions of the Fostering Connections to Success and Increasing Adoptions Act of 2008 became effective on its date of enactment (October 7, 2008). However, a state may have limited additional time to comply with any of the new requirements of the bill, if HHS determines that the state must enact legislation (other than legislation to appropriate funds) in order to meet that requirement(s). As discussed above, the bill stipulates delayed and/or phased in effective dates for its provisions related to removing income eligibility criteria from the federal adoption assistance program (i.e., de-link), extending Title IV-E assistance to eligible youth beyond age 18, providing direct access to tribal entities for federal Title IV-E funding, and providing new or increased federal reimbursement for certain short-term training costs.

Congressional Budget Office Estimates[27]

Although H.R. 6893, as enacted, authorizes significant expansions in federal support for state and tribal child welfare programs, CBO projects a combined change in federal spending and revenues from the overall bill that is roughly budget neutral over ten years (FY2009-FY201 8). Specifically, CBO projects that the bill *will* reduce the federal budget deficit by $15 million over those ten years.[28] This positive effect (i.e. reduction in federal budget deficit) is projected to be much larger in the first five years of the bill's enactment ($449 million), in part because a number of the bill's provisions that are expected to increase federal spending are made effective a year or two after enactment and because the full effect of other provisions is phased in over five or more years.[29]

Projected Savings and Increased Revenue. As interpreted by CBO, four major provisions of the bill are projected to produce significant savings (and/or increase revenues) to the federal treasury over five (FY2009-FY2013) and 10 (FY2009-FY201 8) years. These are as follows:

- authorization of federal Title IV-E support for kinship guardianship assistance (projected to save $60 million over five years and a total of $791 million over 10 years);[30]
- making school enrollment a condition of federal eligibility for foster care, adoption assistance, and kinship guardianship assistance under Title IV-E (projected to save $213 million over five years and a total of $484 million over 10 years);
- new authority to the Treasury Department related to investment of operating cash (projected to save $50 million over five years and a total of $100 million over 10 years); and
- changes to the tax code's uniform definition of qualifying child ($628 million in savings plus $123 million in increased revenue over five years and a total of $1 .402 billion in savings plus a total of $307 million in increased revenue over 10 years).

Projected Increases in Federal Spending. As interpreted by CBO, seven major provisions of the bill are projected to have costs to the federal treasury over the next five (FY2009-FY20 13) and 10 (FY2009-FY200 18) years. A delayed or phased-in implementation of a number of these provisions helps to reduce their projected cost during these time periods. These provisions are as follows:

- annual appropriation of $15 million for Family Connection Grants (projected to increase federal spending by $59 million over five years and by a total of $75 million over 10 years);
- option for states to provide federal Title IV-E assistance up to age 21 for otherwise eligible children remaining in foster care after their 1 8th birthday and for those who left foster care for adoption after attaining age 16 (effective with FY20 11 and projected to increase federal spending by $186 million between that year and FY20 13 and by a total of $735 million between that year and FY20 18);

- expanded child welfare training claims and/or increase in their federal reimbursement rate (the increased reimbursement rate is phased in over FY2009-FY201 3 and is projected to increase federal spending by $138 million over those years and by a total of $412 million over the 10-year period);
- increased oversight of access to health care for children in foster care (projected to increase federal spending by $75 million over 5 years and by a total of $150 million over ten years;
- authority for tribes to apply for and receive direct federal Title IV-E funding (effective with FY20 10 and expected to increase federal spending by $30 million between that year and FY2013 and by a total of $237 million through FY20 18);
- annual appropriation of $3 million for technical assistance and implementation grants related to improving outcomes for Indian children generally, and implementing tribal access to Title IV-E, specifically (projected to increase federal spending by $12 million over 5 years and by a total of $27 million over 10 years); and
- phase out of income (and related) eligibility criteria for federal adoption assistance (phase-out begins with FY2010 and is expected to increase federal spending by $126 million between that year and FY2013 and by a total of $1 .432 billion between that year and FY2018).

ORIGINS OF THE ENACTED BILL AND VIEWS

The Fostering Connections to Success and Increasing Adoptions Act of 2008 (H.R. 6893) was introduced by Representative Jim McDermott, with Representative Jerry Weller, on September 15, 2008, and passed the House (under suspension of the rules and by voice vote) on September 17, 2008. The bill then went to the Senate where it was passed (by unanimous consent) on September 22, 2008. Enacted on October 7, 2008 as P.L. 110-351, the final legislation represented a compromise between bills that were earlier acted on by the House and by the Senate Finance Committee. These bills are the Improved Adoption Incentives and Relative Guardianship Support Act of 2008 (S. 3038) and the Fostering Connections to Success Act (H.R. 6307). S. 3038 was introduced by Senator Grassley in May 2008, and the Senate Finance Committee approved the "Chairman's Mark" version of that bill on September

10, 2008 (S.Rept. 1 10-467).[31] H.R. 6307 was introduced by Representative McDermott with Representative Weller in June 2008, and it passed the House on June 24, 2008.[32] Both Representative McDermott and Representative Weller described the final bill, H.R. 6893, as the product of bipartisan and bicameral legislative work and they cited the importance of Senator Max Baucus and Senator Grassley in this effort.[33]

Congressional Activities

During the first session of the 110th Congress, the Income Security and Family Support Subcommittee of the House Ways and Means Committee held a number of hearings to review challenges facing the child welfare system overall, and, in particular, challenges faced by older youth leaving foster care without a permanent family. Following these hearings, in February 2008, Representative McDermott, who chairs that subcommittee, introduced the Invest in KIDS Act (H.R. 5466) to address a number of these challenges.[34]

Some of the provisions incorporated in H.R. 5466, as well as provisions subsequently included in S. 3038, H.R. 6307, and ultimately those that were included in H.R. 6893, were inspired by, or introduced in, other bills during this and earlier Congresses. From the 110th Congress, these bills include the Kinship Caregiver Support Act (S. 661, introduced by Senator Hillary Clinton with Senator Olympia Snowe / H.R. 2188, introduced by Representative Danny Davis); the Adoption Equality Act (S. 1462, introduced by Senator Jay Rockefeller / H.R. 4091, introduced by Representative Jim Cooper); the Tribal Foster Care and Adoption Access Act (S. 1956, introduced by Senator Max Baucus / H.R. 4688, introduced by Representative Earl Pomeroy); the Foster Care Continuing Opportunities Act (S. 1512, introduced by Senator Barbara Boxer); and a bill to increase reimbursement under Title IV-E for short-term training of private agency workers (H.R. 2314, by Representative Weller).[35]

HHS Views

In providing its view on aspects of earlier bills (H.R. 6307 and the Chairman's Mark of S. 3038), that were subsequently included in the final enrolled bill (H.R. 6893), the U.S. Department of Health and Human Services (HHS) strongly supported revising and extending the Adoption Incentive program but disagreed with (1) the specific ways in which states will now be permitted to seek open-ended federal reimbursement for a part of the cost of providing guardianship subsidies to eligible children leaving foster care; (2) the creation of Family Connection grants; and (3) the approach taken in providing access to federal Title IV-E support for tribes.[36] In letters sent to Congress regarding H.R. 6307 and the Chairman's Mark of S. 3038, HHS, however, did not provide any specific comments related to the expansion of federal eligibility for Title IV-E adoption assistance, the option for states to continue providing federal Title IV-E foster care assistance to eligible youth after their 18th birthday, nor regarding the provisions related to increased federal reimbursement for certain child welfare training costs.

With regard to the state option to provide guardianship assistance under Title IV-E, HHS wrote: "Moving children to permanent homes as expeditiously as possible is an important goal. However, we oppose creating a new entitlement under the title IV-E program for subsidized relative guardians."[37] HHS noted that under the Child Welfare Program Option it has proposed, states would have the "flexibility to support guardianship agreements if they choose."[38] HHS also noted its support for direct federal support to tribes for child welfare programs but, again, it preferred the approach that would be provided to tribes under the Child Welfare Program Option. (The Bush Administration's proposed program option would permit federally recognized tribes to receive child welfare funds from a fixed sum that would be set aside for that purpose.) The Department wrote that it had "serious concerns" that the bills would "weaken [child protection] requirements placed on Tribes in comparison to those placed on States."[39] Finally, in the letter regarding H.R. 6307, HHS pointed out that the activities allowed under the Family Connection Grants could already be funded under existing Title IV-B programs (Child Welfare Services, and Promoting Safe and Stable Families) and also that the Department does not support any new "authorization of activities outside the President's Budget."[40]

Bill Advocates and Support

The act responds to a variety of issues that have been raised for many years (and some for more than a decade) by public child welfare administrators; child welfare, youth, adoption, and tribal advocates; and children and youth who have been (or still are) in foster care; and/or by public child welfare administrators. Enactment of the Fostering Connections to

Success and Increasing Adoptions Act of 2008 was urged by many groups, including a coalition of 581 national, state, and local entities (representing organizations in all 50 states) that advocate on behalf of children and youth, as well as by the National Conference of State Legislators (NCSL) and the Conference of Chief Justices and Conference of State Court Administrators.[41]

Section-by-Section Description of the Bill

The Fostering Connections to Success and Increasing Adoptions Act of 2008 (P.L. 110-351) is divided into six titles, most with multiple sections, and makes the following changes.

Title I: Connecting and Supporting Relative Caregivers

Section 101: Kinship Guardianship Assistance Payment For Children

- *Permits states to claim federal reimbursement (under Title IV-E) for a part of the cost of providing kinship guardianship assistance* to every eligible child who leaves foster care for placement with a grandparent or other relative who has chosen to become the child's legal guardian.
- Requires that *to be eligible* for federal kinship guardianship assistance *a child must have been eligible to receive federal foster care maintenance payments while living for no less then six consecutive months in the home of his or her prospective relative guardian* (this effectively requires that the prospective relative guardian has met the state foster family home licensing standards and prospective foster parent background checks).
- Stipulates the following additional conditions of federal eligibility for kinship guardianship assistance: The state must determine that (1) the child has been removed from his or her home through a voluntary placement agreement or because a judge found that home contrary to the child's welfare; (2) neither being reunited with his or her parents nor adoption are appropriate permanency options for the child; (3) the child demonstrates a strong attachment to the prospective relative

guardian and the relative guardian has a strong commitment to caring permanently for the child; and (4) any child age 14 or older was consulted before being placed in the kinship guardianship arrangement.

- Provides also that the state must have specific background checks procedures for relative guardians, including fingerprint-based checks of national crime databases and child abuse and neglect registry checks, which must be conducted before a relative guardian may receive kinship guardianship assistance payments on behalf of an eligible child.
- Permits states to place a sibling(s) of an eligible child in the same kinship guardianship arrangement and to make kinship guardianship assistance payments on behalf of the sibling(s).
- Establishes that a *kinship guardianship assistance payment* made on behalf of an eligible child *must not be more than the amount the child would receive as a foster care* maintenance payment if he or she remained in a foster family home.
- *Ensures continued categorical Medicaid eligibility* for children receiving federal kinship guardianship assistance.
- Provides that to *receive federal reimbursement for kinship guardianship assistance payments, the state must enter into a written and binding kinship guardianship agreement with the prospective relative guardian*, which must stipulate that it will remain in effect without regard to the state in which the relative guardian lives and must include (1) the amount of, and manner in which, the kinship guardianship assistance payments will be made on the child's behalf, including the manner in which the amount may, in consultation with the relative guardian, be adjusted periodically based on the circumstances of the relative and the needs of the child; and (2) the additional services and assistance the child and relative will be eligible for under the agreement, including the procedure the relative guardian may use to apply for additional services as needed.
- Entitles each state to claim federal reimbursement for the cost of providing kinship guardianship assistance payments on behalf of an eligible child at the same federal reimbursement rate that is provided for adoption assistance (i.e., ranges from 50%-83%, based on each state's Federal Medical Assistance Percentage, FMAP); and entitles state to claim federal reimbursement of 50% for (non-training)

administrative costs related to providing kinship guardianship assistance to eligible children.

- Further stipulates that the kinship guardianship assistance agreement must provide that the state will pay the total nonrecurring expenses *associated with obtaining legal guardianship of the child, or $2,000 of those expenses, whichever is less.*
- For any child in foster care whose permanency plan is placement with a relative guardian and receipt of kinship guardianship assistance payments, requires states to describe in the child's written case plan the (1) steps the agency has taken to determine that it is not appropriate for the child to be returned home or adopted; (2) reasons why a permanent placement in a kinship guardianship assistance arrangement is in the child's best interests; (3) reasons for any separation from siblings during the placement; (4) efforts the state has made to discuss adoption with the relative foster parent, and, if adoption is not chosen by the relative foster parent, documentation of reasons why this is so; and (5) efforts made by the state to discuss with the child's parent or parents, the kinship guardianship arrangement or reasons why the efforts were not made; and (6) the ways in which the child meets the eligibility criteria for kinship guardianship assistance.
- At the termination of any state child welfare demonstration project (waiver) that is related to guardianship and was authorized by the U.S. Department of Health and Human Services (HHS) under Section 1130 of the Social Security Act, provides that the state's costs of providing assistance or services to any child being served under such a demonstration project, as of September 30, 2008, continue to be eligible for federal reimbursement under Title IV-E — but only to the extent that the services and assistance are provided to such a child under the same terms and conditions that applied during the demonstration project.
- *Authorizes states to use federal funds under the Chafee Foster Care Independence Program to provide independent living services and other supports to youth who — after reaching their 16th birthday — leave foster care for adoption or placement in kinship guardianship* and permit youth leaving foster care for kinship guardianship after reaching their 1 6th birthday to be eligible for Education and Training Vouchers. (Children who leave foster care for adoption after their 1

6th birthday continue to be eligible for Education and Training Vouchers under current law.)

Section 102: Family Connection Grants

- *Appropriates mandatory funding of $15 million* (for each of FY2009-FY2013) for Family Connection Grants (to be awarded on a competitive basis to public (state, local, or tribal) child welfare agencies or eligible private, non-profit organizations) for the support of one or more of the following: *kinship navigator programs, intensive family-finding efforts that utilize search technology to find biological relatives, family group decision-making meetings*, which, when appropriate, must safely address issues of domestic violence; and *residential family treatment centers that enable parents and children to live together in a safe environment* for no less than six months and that provide a full range of services to meet the family's needs (onsite or by referral), including substance abuse treatment services, children's early intervention services, family counseling, medical and mental health services, nursery and pre-school, and other services designed to support the family.
- *Requires HHS to annually award no less than $5 million* of the Family Connections Grants funds to *support of kinship navigator programs*, that, through information referral systems and other means, assist kinship caregivers in learning about, finding, and using programs and services to meet their own needs and those of the children they are raising, and promote effective partnerships among public and private agencies to ensure these kinship caregiver families are served.
- Requires HHS to set aside no less than 3% of the total annual funding for Family Connection grants for evaluation of grantee activities; and permits HHS to set-aside 2% of total funding for the grants for technical assistance to grantees.
- Provides that HHS may make no more than 30 new Family Connection grants each year; may not award these grants for less than one year nor more than three years; and that it must provide 75% of the funding for a grantee's approved program costs in the first and second year of the grant and 50% in the third year.

- Renames Title IV-B, Subpart 1 of the Social Security Act (which is now named "Child Welfare Services") as the "Stephanie Tubbs Jones Child Welfare Services Program."

Section 103: Notification of Relatives

- *Requires states (under Title IV-E), within 30 days of removing a child from the custody of his or her parent(s) to exercise due diligence to identify all adult grandparents and other adult relatives of the child and to provide them with (1) notice of the child's removal from parental custody; (2) an explanation of their options for participating in the care and placement of the child;* (3) a description of the requirements that must be met to be a licensed foster family home and the additional services and support for children placed in licensed homes; and (4) if state has opted to provide kinship guardianship assistance, a description of how the relative can enter into a kinship guardianship assistance agreement; this requirement is subject to exceptions due to family or domestic violence.

Section 104: Licensing Standards for Relatives

- *Codifies* (under Title IV-E) *existing federal guidance permitting states to waive "non-safety" licensing standards (as determined by the state) for relative foster family caregivers*, but only on a *case-bycase basis* and for a specific child in care.
- *Requires HHS to prepare and submit* to the Senate Finance Committee and the House Ways and Means Committee a *report on licensing of relative foster family homes, including* (1) the number and percentage of children living in licensed relative foster family homes and those living in unlicensed relative foster family homes; (2) the frequency with which states grant waivers of "non-safety" standards and the type of non-safety standards waived; (3) an assessment of how the use of such waivers have affected safety, permanence, and well-being outcomes for children in foster care; (4) a review of any reasons why relative foster family homes may remain unlicensed despite this waiver authority; and (5) recommendations for administrative or

legislative actions to increase the share of relative foster family homes that are licensed while ensuring the safety of foster children and improving their permanence and well-being.

Section 105: Authority for Comparisons and Disclosures of Information in the Federal Parent Locator Service

- Permits state child welfare agencies more direct access to the Federal Parent Locator Service.

Title II. Improving Outcomes for Children in Foster Care

Section 201: State Option for Children in Foster Care, and Certain Children in An Adoptive or Guardianship Placement, After Attaining Age 18

- *Permits states (as of October 1, 2010) to extend federal (Title IV-E) assistance to an eligible child after his or her 18th birthday if the child is in foster care under the responsibility of the state* or if the child left foster care for federal adoption or guardianship assistance after reaching his or her 16th birthday, *provided the child* has not yet reached his or her 21st birthday and is in school, employed (at least 80 hours a month), *in another activity designed to promote, or remove barriers to employment*, or is incapable of participating in any of those activities because of a documented medical condition.
- *Except in the case of the individuals described above, defines the term "child" as an individual under the age of 18 for all federal child welfare programs included in the Social Security Act* (i.e., Child Welfare Services, Promoting Safe and Stable Families, Foster Care and Adoption Assistance, and Chafee Foster Care Independence Program).
- Also permits children in foster care who are age 18 or older to retain eligibility for federal foster care maintenance payments while living independently in a supervised setting (as must be defined in regulations by HHS).

- Further permits states to continue federal kinship guardianship assistance up to age 21 for a child who has a mental or physical handicap that the state determines warrants this continued assistance (This was previously, and continues to be, the law with regard to provision of federal adoption assistance.)
- Prohibits payment of federal kinship guardianship assistance payments to a relative guardian if the relative guardian is no longer legally responsible for support of the child (who is under age 18) or if the state determines that the child is no longer receiving support from the relative guardian. (This was previously, and continues to be, the law with regard to adoptive parents and children receiving federal adoption assistance.)
- Makes October 1, 2010, the effective date for all the amendments made in this section (Section 201).

Section 202: Transition Plan for Children Aging Out of Foster Care

- *Requires states* (under Title IV-E) *to have procedures to ensure that 90 days before a child in foster care reaches his or her 18th birthday* (or 90 days before the later birthday up to which a state elects to provide Title IV-E foster care assistance), *the child's caseworker and other representatives* (as appropriate) *must work with the child to develop a personal transition plan* that includes specific options on housing, health insurance, education, local opportunities for mentors and continuing support services, and workforce supports and employment services.

Section 203: Short-term Training for Child Welfare Agencies, Relative Guardians, and Court Personnel

- *Allows states to claim federal reimbursement of the costs of providing short-term training* — related to carrying out the Title IV- E foster care, adoption and kinship guardianship assistance program — *to current or prospective relative guardians, staff of state- licensed or state-approved (private) child welfare agencies, and for certain court or court-related personnel handling abuse and neglect cases.*

- *Phases in a 75% federal reimbursement rate* for these relative guardian, private child welfare agency workers, and court or court-related personnel training claims beginning at 55% in FY2009 and rising by 5% annually (until the reimbursement rate reaches 75% for all Title IV-E eligible training costs in FY2013).

Section 204: Educational Stability

- Restates current requirement (under Title IV-E) that the state must assure that a child's foster care placement takes into account the appropriateness of the child's current educational setting and the proximity of that placement to the school in which the child is enrolled at the time.
- *Requires states to assure that they have coordinated with appropriate local educational agencies to ensure that the child remains in the school in which he or she is enrolled* at the time of the placement, or, if this is not in the child's best interests, to assure (with the local educational agencies) *that the child will be immediately and appropriately enrolled in a new school* with all of the education records of the child provided to the school.
- *Permits a state to claim federal reimbursement* at the state's Federal Medical Assistance Percentage or FMAP, which ranges from 50%-83% based on state per capita income) *for the cost of transporting a child to the school in which he or she was enrolled at the time of foster care placement.*
- *Requires a state to provide assurances that each school-age child who receives federal* (Title IV-E) *assistance* (whether in foster care, kinship guardianship or adoption) *is enrolled in school full-time*, or has already completed high school.

Section 205: Health Oversight and Coordination Plan

- *Requires each state* (under Title IV-B) — working through the state child welfare agency and the state agency that administers Medicaid and in consultation with pediatricians, other health care experts, and experts in, and recipients of, child welfare services — *to create a plan to ensure oversight and coordination of health care, for children in foster care; the plan must include a strategy to identify and respond to the health care needs of children in foster care, including their mental health and dental health needs*, and provide an outline of (1) the schedule for initial and follow-up health screens; (2) how health needs identified in these screens will be monitored and treated; (3) how medical information for children in care will be updated and appropriately shared, which may include development of an electronic health record; (4) steps to ensure continuity of health care services, which may include establishment of a medical home for every child in care; (5) oversight of prescription medicines; and (6) how the state actively consults with and involves physicians and other appropriate medical or nonmedical professionals in assessing the health and well-being of children in foster care and in determining appropriate medical treatment for them.

- Stipulates that this requirement must not be understood to reduce or limit responsibility of the state Medicaid agency to administer and provide care and services to children served by the state child welfare agency under the Child Welfare Services program (Title IV- B, Subpart 1).

Section 206: Sibling Placement

- *Requires each state (under Title IV-E) to make reasonable efforts to place siblings removed from their home in the same foster care, kinship guardianship, or adoptive placement*, unless the state can document that joint placement is contrary to the safety or well-being of any of the siblings.
- *In the case of siblings who are not jointly placed, requires states to provide for "frequent visitation or other ongoing interaction between the siblings*," unless the state documents that this would be contrary to the safety or well-being of any of the siblings.

TITLE III: TRIBAL FOSTER CARE AND ADOPTION ACCESS

Section 301: Equitable Access for Foster Care and Adoption Services for Indian Children in Tribal Areas

- *Permits (as of October 1, 2009) an Indian tribe, tribal organization, or tribal consortium with an approved Title IV-E plan to make claims for federal reimbursement of eligible foster care maintenance, adoption assistance, or kinship guardianship assistance payments* and for related child placement and administrative costs (including those for data collection and training) made on behalf of eligible children who are under tribal responsibility.
- For purposes of defining the tribal entities that may apply for direct federal Title IV-E funding, generally defines "Indian tribe" as any federally recognized tribe, a "tribal organization" as the recognized governing body of any such tribe, and describes a tribal consortium as any two or more Indian tribes or tribal organizations that together submit a single Title IV-E plan for approval.[42]
- With limited and specific exceptions, *requires tribes seeking direct federal support under Title IV-E to meet all the requirements of Title IV-E "in the same manner" as they must be met by a state* receiving these funds.
- *Provides for calculation of a tribe-specific federal matching rate for foster care maintenance payments, adoption assistance payments, and kinship guardianship assistance payments* (a "tribal FMAP"); provides that tribes with an approved Title IV-E plan receive this reimbursement rate directly from the federal government; also provides that if the tribe has a cooperative agreement or contract with a state to administer IV-E payments, the federal government must pay the state the tribal matching rate for the payments made under that agreement.
- Stipulates that any currently existing cooperative agreement or contract entered into between a tribe and state for the administration or payment of funds under Title IV-E must remain in effect after the enactment of this bill, subject to the right of either party to revoke or modify the terms of the agreement or contract, and, further, that states and tribes may continue to enter into agreements or contracts under Title IV-E.

- Permits tribal entities seeking to administer independent living services for eligible Indian children and youth to apply to HHS for an allotment of funds under the Chafee Foster Care Independence Program (and/or for an allotment of Education and Training Voucher funds); and provides that successful tribal applicants are to receive an allotment amount(s) out of the state's allotment for the program(s) that is based on the share of all children in foster care in that state who are under the authority of that tribal entity.
- Stipulates specific parameters within which tribes with an approved Title IV-E plan may (for a limited time — unless extended by regulation or law) claim federal reimbursement, under that plan, for in-kind expenditures from third-party sources; requires HHS (no later than September 30, 2011) to issue regulations related to this kind of Title IV-E claiming by tribes.
- *Requires (as of October 1, 2009) a state, under its Title IV-E state plan, to negotiate in good faith with any tribal entity in the state that seeks an agreement with the state to administer all or part of the Title IV-E program on behalf of the Indian children* who are under the authority of the tribal entity; and similarly requires as of that date a state, under the Chafee Foster Care Independence Program, to negotiate in good faith with any tribal entity in the state that does not receive a direct federal allotment of Chafee funds if that tribal entity seeks an agreement or contract with the state to administer, supervise, or oversee the program on behalf of eligible Indian children under the tribal entity's authority.
- *Require HHS, in consultation with tribal entities and affected states, to issue interim final regulations no later than October 7, 2009*, to implement the tribal access provisions; provides further that these regulations must ensure that a transfer of responsibility for the placement and care of a child from a state child welfare agency to a tribal child welfare agency effects neither the child's eligibility for Title IV-E or Medicaid nor the services or payments provided to the child under those parts of the law; (adds that the regulations must ensure this is the case whether the child is transferred to a tribe that is operating its program under an approved Title IV-E plan or under a cooperative agreement with a state).
- Makes October 1,2009 (first day of FY2010) the effective date for most provisions in this section (Section 301). However, requirements in this section related to HHS regulations and certain "rules of

construction" were effective with the date of enactment, October 7, 2008.

Section 302: Technical Assistance and Implementation

- *To improve services and permanency outcomes for Indian children and their families, requires HHS to provide technical assistance to tribes and states* regarding tribal administration of child welfare programs and required state-tribe interactions related to serving Indian children; and *implementation grants to tribes that are preparing a Title IV-E plan for approval*, which must not be valued at more than $300,000 and must be used to develop data collection systems, cost allocation plans, agency and tribal court procedures necessary to meet the case review requirements, or any other costs attributable to meeting any other requirement necessary for approval of a Title IV-E plan.
- Stipulates that an implementation grant must only be made to a tribal entity one-time and that as a condition of receiving the grant the tribal entity must agree to repay the total amount of the grant if it does not submit a Title IV-E plan to HHS for approval within 24 months of receiving the funds; (the repayment requirement must be waived by HHS if "circumstances beyond the control" of the tribe prevent its submission of a plan within 24 months).
- *Appropriates $3 million annually* (beginning with FY2009) for this technical assistance and implementation grants and permits HHS to provide this assistance and service either directly or through a grant or contract with a public or private organization knowledgeable in Indian tribal affairs and child welfare.

TITLE IV : IMPROVEMENT OF INCENTIVES FOR ADOPTION

Section 401: Adoption Incentives Program

- *Extends funding authority for Adoption Incentives for five years* (FY2009-FY2013) at $43 million annually; resets the base number of adoptions a state needs to finalize to earn an incentive award (in each of FY2008-FY2012) to the number it finalized in FY2007; raises the incentive amount available for an increase in the number of older child adoptions (from $4,000 to $8,000) and for special needs (younger than age nine) adoptions (from $2,000 to $4,000); continues prior law incentive payment amount of $4,000 for increase in overall number of children adopted from foster care; and ensures that states have 24 months to spend any Adoption Incentive awards earned.

- *Requires that any appropriated Adoption Incentive funds not needed to make awards for an increase in the number of adoptions finalized, must be paid as incentive awards for any state that increases the rate at which children are adopted from foster care*; to earn this award for adoptions finalized in any of FY2008 through FY2012 a state must achieve a "foster child adoption rate" that exceeds its previous "highest ever foster child adoption rate" (beginning with FY2002); the amount of the award is $1,000 times the increased number of adoptions achieved by the state that are attributed to the increased adoption rate.[43]

Section 402: Promotion of Adoption of Children with Special Needs

- Phases in (based on age, length of stay in care and membership in sibling group) *elimination of all income, resource, and family structure tests associated with eligibility for federal Title IV-E adoption assistance*, including such tests that were established as part of the prior law cash aid program, which was known as Aid to Families with Dependent Children (AFDC).
- *Begins the phase in of these revised adoption assistance eligibility criteria in FY2010 for any child who is age 16 or older* at the time his or her adoption assistance agreement is finalized (in that or a later year) and *gradually lower this age, until FY2018, when the new eligibility rules will apply to a child of any age.*
- Provides that *as of FY2010 the revised adoption assistance eligibility criteria also applies to any child who has been in care for 60, or more, consecutive months* at the time the adoption assistance agreement is finalized, without regard to the child's age at that time.

- Further stipulates that *as of FY2010 the revised adoption assistance eligibility criteria also apply to any child who is a sibling of a child for whom the new eligibility rules are effective* (whether because of that child's age or length of stay in care), provided that the sibling will be placed in the same adoptive home as the child for whom the new eligibility rules apply.

Section 403: Information on Adoption Tax Credit

- Requires states to provide information to individuals who are adopting a child from foster care, and to those who the state learns are considering such an adoption, of their potential eligibility for the federal adoption tax credit.

TITLE V: CLARIFICATION OF UNIFORM DEFINITION OF CHILD AND OTHER PROVISIONS

[*The provisions of this Title are not a part of federal child welfare policy but are changes made to other parts of federal law, including the tax code, to offset costs of increased federal child welfare spending authorized in the previous titles of the enacted bill.*]

Section 501: Clarification of Uniform Definition of Child

- Clarifies the uniform definition of qualifying child under the Internal Revenue Code (1) for purposes of the dependency exemption, the child credit, the earned income credit, the dependent care credit, and head of household filing status, to ensure that such an individual is unmarried and is younger than the taxpayer claiming the individual on his/her tax return; (2) for purposes of the child credit, provide that a qualifying child must be the dependent of the taxpayer claiming the credit; and (3) provide that if a taxpayer claiming a qualifying child is not the parent of the individual so claimed, he or she must have an adjusted gross income that is higher than either of the child's parents.

Section 502: Investment of Operating Cash

- In addition to the current investment options, permits the Treasury Department to invest excess operating cash for 90 days in repurchase agreements.

Section 503: No Federal Funding to Unlawfully Present Individuals

- Prohibits any interpretation of the bill that would "alter" any current "prohibitions on Federal payments to individuals who are unlawfully present in the United States."

TITLE VI : EFFECTIVE DATE

Unless a different date is stipulated in the Fostering Connections to Success and Increasing Adoptions Act of 2008, the effective date of the amendments made by the bill is October 7, 2008 (date of its enactment); for any state, permits a time-limited exception to the effective date of any requirement added by this bill (under Title IV-B or Title IV-E) if HHS determines that the state must enact legislation (other than legislation to appropriate funds) to comply with a new requirement.

End Notes

[1] For more information on the these earlier bills, see the subsection, "Origins of the Enacted Bill and Views" later this report.

[2] This report seeks to provide a "plain" language discussion of the bill. However, certain child welfare provisions may be subject to different interpretations. HHS has the authority to implement these provisions and, in doing this, will interpret their meaning.

[3] Section 47 5(7) of the Social Security Act.

[4] For programs implemented in place as of 2004, see Children's Defense Fund, *State's Subsidized Guardianship Laws at a Glance,* (October 2004).

[5] Congress initially granted child welfare "waiver" authority to HHS (P.L. 103-432, 1994) That authority is currently expired, although some states continued to operate assisted guardianship programs with Title IV-E dollars under previously approved waivers. As of September 30, 2008, the seven state believed to have ongoing demonstration projects (waivers) specifically addressing guardianship were IL, IA, MN, MT, OR, TN, and WI. See

James Bell Associates, "Summary of the Title IV-E Child Welfare Waiver Demonstrations," June 2008.

6 U.S. Department of Health and Human Services, *Synthesis of Findings, Assisted Guardianship: Child Welfare Waiver Demonstrations*, September 2005.

7 Pew Commission on Children in Foster Care, *Fostering the Future: Safety, Permanence and Well-Being for Children in Foster Care*, May 2004, p. 16; U.S. Government Accountability Office (GAO), *African American Children in Foster Care: Additional HHS Assistance Needed to Hel States Reduce the Proportion in Care*, July 2007, p. 6.

8 See S.Rept. 110-467 to accompany S. 3038, p. 5. These reasons are similar to those given for the creation of the adoption assistance program in 1980 (P.L. 96-272). See U.S. Congress, Senate, 96th Congress, 1st session, *Adoption Assistance and Child Welfare Amendments of 1979*, S.Rept. 96-336, p. 13 and U.S. Congress, House of Representatives, 96th Congress, 1st session, *Social Services and Child Welfare Amendments of 1979*, H.Rept. 96-136, p. 55-56.

9 Regarding past legislative actions related to both kinship placement and guardianship under Title IV-E of the Social Security Act, see "Placement with Relatives and Guardianship," in U.S. Congress, Senate, 110th Congress, 2nd session, *Improved Adoption Incentives and Relative Guardianship Support Act of 2008*, S.Rept. 110-467, p. 2-3 [http://frwebgate.access 1 0_cong_reports&docid=f :sr467.1 10.pdf].

10 The enacted bill stipulates that this requirement is subject to exceptions due to family or domestic violence.

11 The FPLS was created initially for child support enforcement purposes and only noncustodial parents of the child may be identified by name match. However, this information may also help to locate additional relatives. Under prior law states could seek information from the FPLS indirectly (through the state child support agency) rather than directly from HHS. For more information, see U.S. Department of Health and Human Services (HHS), Administration for Children and Families (ACF) Information Memorandum, "Appropriate Referrals, Requests for Location Services, Child Support Applications, and Electronic Interface between Child Welfare and Child Support Enforcement Agencies,"ACYF-CB-IM-07-06 (issued jointly with the Office of Child Support Enforcement), September 7, 2007 [http://www.acf.hhs.gov/programs/cb/laws

12 P.L. 110-351 does not specify how the state's "savings" are to be determined and it is not exactly clear how this requirement will be implemented.

13 For purposes of the Title IV-E adoption assistance program, to qualify as a child with "special needs," the state must have determined that (1) the child cannot or should not be returned to the home of his/her parents; (2) that there is a factor or condition specific to the child (such as the child's age, membership in sibling group, race/ethnicity, medical condition, or a physical, emotional or mental disability) that makes it "reasonable to conclude" that the child will not be adopted without adoption assistance or Medicaid. Further, unless this is not in the child's best interest (e.g. because of significant bonding with foster parents), the state must determine that reasonable, but unsuccessful, efforts to place the child without such assistance have been made. See Section 473(c) of the Social Security Act.

14 In certain instances, the home from which the child is removed might also be the home of another relative caretaker. Regarding the creation and evolution of the link between eligibility for federal cash welfare assistance, see "Title IV-E Foster Care and Adoption Assistance," in S.Rept. 110-467, p. 2, accompanying S. 3038.

15 Many observers and stakeholders also believe this link is inappropriate for determining eligibility for federal foster care maintenance payments under Title IV-E. However, consensus on how to change this policy has not been reached. P.L. 110-351 leaves the link between federal foster care eligibility and the rules of the now repealed AFDC program in place, and, by making eligibility for federal foster care maintenance payments a pre-condition of eligibility for federal kinship guardianship assistance, it indirectly establishes this link with regard to the new kinship guardianship assistance program. For more information on the link, see CRS Report RL34388, *Child Welfare Issues in the 110th*

Congress, especially the section "Delink Foster Care and Adoption Assistance from AFDC Rules" and Appendix A, by Emilie Stoltzfus.

16 These FY2007 award amounts were determined in the last quarter of FY2008. However, available appropriated funds for Adoption Incentives (just over $9 million) were not sufficient to provide the full FY2007 award amounts at that time. HHS indicated its intent to pay a part of the FY2007 awards (roughly 84%) at the end of FY2008 and the remainder (roughly 16%) at the beginning of FY2009. See Adoption Incentive award history table at [http://www.acf.hhs.gov/programs/cb/programs_fund/adopt_incentive_history.htm].

17 In its FY2009 Budget, the Bush Administration proposed fixing the Adoption Incentive baseline year as FY2007 and increasing award amounts for older and special needs adoptions. The enacted bill (H.R. 6893) adopted these proposals (although it increased the award amounts differently), added others (e.g., incentive for increase in rate) but did not adopt another Administration proposal to limit state use of any earned incentive award funds for finalizing adoption or other permanency options. For more information see CRS Report RL34388, "Adoption Incentives" in *Child Welfare Issues in the 110th Congress*, by Emilie Stoltzfus.

18 For a description of how to calculate this award see the footnote on this question that is included under "Section: 401: Adoption Incentives Program," near the end of the report.

19 For more information on the adoption tax credit, see CRS Report RL33633, *Tax Benefits for Families: Adoption,* by Christine Scott.

20 For more legislative history on this issue see S.Rept. 110-467, p. 4, accompanying S. 3038 and for a comprehensive look at the issue of youth aging out of foster care see CRS Report RL3 4499, *Youth Transitioning from Foster Care: Background, Federal Programs, and Issues for Congress,* by Adrienne Fernandes.

21 For additional information regarding living arrangements for older youth, see CRS Report RL3 4499, *Youth Transitioning from Foster Care: Background, Federal Programs, and Issues for Congress,* by Adrienne Fernandes.

22 The assertion of safety, permanency, and well-being as primary federal child welfare policy goals was first introduced by the Clinton Administration as part of implementing new funding for family preservation and family support services (authorized in 1993 by P.L. 103- 66). Before 2006 then, the sole *statutory* use of the term "well-being" in Title IV-B and Title IV-E — and as distinct from safety, permanence or child "welfare" — was a reference added by that 1993 law as part of the definition of "family support." (Although it is commonly cited as establishing safety, permanency, and *well-being,* as the primary federal child welfare goals, the Adoption and Safe Families Act (P.L. 105-89, 1997) focused on safety and permanence and did not add the term "well-being" to the statute.) The 109th Congress, however, added "well-being" to Title IV-B and Title IV-E in several places. Notably, P.L. 109-288 (2006) restated the purposes of Title IV-B, subpart 1 to include "promoting the safety, permanence, and well-being of children in foster care and adoptive families." (For early discussion of "well-being" of children and families as a primary federal child welfare policy goal see U.S. Department of Health and Human Services, Administration for Children and Families, ACYF-PI-94-0 1, January 18, 1994; *Federal Register*, October 4, 1994, p. 50646-50673 and *Federal Register,* November 18, 1996, p. 58657.)

23 This means states are now *statutorily* entitled to, in most cases, a higher federal reimbursement rate for these transportation costs than was permitted by federal guidance issued on this topic in December 2007. That *guidance* clarified that states could claim reimbursement of 50% for these transportation costs. (See U.S. Department of Health and Human Services, Administration for Children and Families, Children's Bureau, *Child Welfare Policy Manual*, Section 8. 1B, Question 27.)

24 For many years states have been required to collect "to the extent available and accessible" the health and education record of each child in foster care (as part of each child's case plan) and to take into account the proximity of the school in which a child was enrolled when

placing a child in foster care. The 1 09th Congress enacted two changes that moved Congress in the direction of the 2008 requirements: (1) it removed the modifying phrase "to the extent available and accessible," leaving simply the requirement that states collect the health and education records of children in foster care (P.L. 109-239), and (2) it added a new requirement that states must consult with physicians on appropriate care for children in foster care (P.L. 109-288).

[25] S.Rept. 110-467, accompanying S. 3038, p. 5.

[26] The definitions of "Indian tribe" and "tribal organization" included in P.L. 110-351 are the same as those included in Section 4 of the Indian Self Determination and Education Assistance Act and generally extend the authority to apply for these funds to all federally recognized tribes, as well as, the recognized governing body of those tribes. In addition, a "tribal consortium," including two or more tribes or tribal organizations acting together, may apply for direct federal funding under Title IV-E.

[27] Projections in this section are from Congressional Budget Office (CBO), *Preliminary Estimates of Foster Care/Adoption Assistance Draft,* September 15, 2008.

[28] In the event of a federal surplus, the bill projects an *increase in that* surplus of $15 million.

[29] Over the first five years (FY2009-FY20 13), CBO projects that the bill will reduce federal spending by $326 million, plus increase revenues by $123 million, for a reduction in the budget deficit of $449 million (or an increase in any budget surplus by that amount).

[30] CBO included any expected effect of the policy permitting states to extend federal eligibility for kinship guardianship assistance to age 21 (for otherwise eligible children leaving foster care for kinship guardianship at age 16 or older) in this estimate.

[31] As introduced in May 2008, S. 3038 included provisions primarily related to reauthorizing the Adoption Incentives program, delinking federal adoption assistance from income and related eligibility criteria, and supporting guardianship assistance under Title IV-E. The bill approved by the Senate Finance Committee on September 10, 2008, was the Chairman's Mark version of S. 3038 (brought by Senator Max Baucus), which was offered as a complete substitute to the original bill. The Chairman's Mark largely maintained the provisions included in the introduced bill while adding provisions related to direct tribal access to Title IV-E funding, continued Title IV-E eligibility for youth after age 18, transition planning for youth leaving foster care, a licensing demonstration project, and others . (See S.Rept. 110-467.)

[32] H.R. 6307 was based in large part on the provision of Title IV of an earlier bill introduced by Representative McDermott in February 2008, the Invest in KIDS Act (H.R. 5466). The Subcommittee on Income Security and Family Support of the House Ways and Means Committee (Chaired by Representative McDermott) held a hearing in late February 2008 at which it received testimony on the provisions of H.R. 5466. In his prepared opening remarks, Representative Weller noted certain areas of agreement and disagreement with H.R. 5466 and asserted that "we should work together to identify provisions that have bipartisan support so we can get something done this year."

[33] *Congressional Record,* September 17, 2008, p. H83 17.

[34] See CRS Report RL34388, *Child Welfare Issues in the 110th Congress*, by Emilie Stoltzfus.

[35] See Statement of Representative McDermott, *Congressional Record*, September 17, 2008, p. H83 17 and Senate Finance Committee, News Release, Statement of Senator Max Baucus, Chairman, Finance Committee, "Executive Session to Consider Adoption Incentive, Elder Justice, and Patient Safety Proposals," September 10, 2008.

[36] Letter to Honorable Max Baucus, Chairman, Committee on Finance, U.S. Senate, (including the Department's views on the Chairman's amendment in the nature of a substitute for S. 3038, the Improved Adoption Incentives and Relative Guardianship Support Act of 2008), from Mike Leavitt, Secretary, U.S. Department of Health and Human Services (HHS), September 9, 2008; and Letter to Honorable Charles B. Rangel, Chairman, Committee on Ways and Means, U.S. House of Representatives, (including the Department's views on H.R. 6307, the Fostering Connections to Success Act) from Mike Leavitt, Secretary, U.S.

Department of Health and Human Services (HHS), June 24, 2008. Both letters were provided to the Congressional Research Services (CRS) by the U.S. Department of Health and Human Services (HHS).

[37] Ibid. Identical language in both letters.

[38] Beginning with its FY2003 budget the Bush Administration has annually proposed the Child Welfare Program Option. However, no legislative language has been publicly offered to implement the proposal. According to Budget documents, under this option states could elect to receive Title IV-E foster care funds as a lump sum (capped) and, further, to use those funds for the full range of child welfare purposes and in support of any child. For more information see CRS Report RL34388, *Child Welfare Issues in the 110th Congress,* "Appendix A," by Emilie Stoltzfus.

[39] Language quoted is identical in both letters (see cite above). However, the letter regarding H.R. 6307 provides examples of specific provisions HHS believes would weaken provisions for Indian children (alternative background checks for tribes, and broad permission for HHS to waive Title IV-E requirements if requested by the tribe). Those specific provisions were not included in the Chairman's Mark of S. 3038 and, subsequently, were not included in H.R. 6893, as enacted.

[40] Family Connection Grants were not authorized in the Chairman's Mark of S. 3038 and are not discussed in this letter.

[41] See letters of support inserted in the *Congressional Record,* September 17, 2008, H83 16-H8317.

[42] The specific definitions of "Indian tribe" and "tribal organization" are as those terms are defined in Section 4 of the Indian Self-Determination and Education Assistance Act.

[43] To calculate the number of adoptions that are attributed to an increase in the adoption rate you must know the state's "foster child adoption rate" in the award year, the number of children in the state's foster care caseload on the last day of the fiscal year just prior to the award year, and the state's "highest ever foster child adoption rate." A state's foster child adoption rate must be determined by dividing the number of foster child adoptions finalized in the state in a given fiscal year by the number of children in that state's foster care caseload on the last day of the previous year. For example, if a state finalizes 150 adoption during FY2008 and on the last day of the previous fiscal year (September 30, 2007) it had 1,500 children in foster care then the state's foster child adoption rate for FY2008 is equal to 10%. That state earns an award for adoptions in FY2008 if this foster child adoption rate (10%) is above its "highest ever foster child adoption rate" — meaning the best foster child adoption rate the state has ever previously achieved beginning with FY2002. For example, if the highest ever foster child adoption rate the state in the example above had achieved before FY2008 was 9%, then for FY2008, the state's adoption incentive award amount based on the rate increase would be calculated as follows: Multiplying that highest ever rate (9%) by the 1,500 children in care on the last day of the fiscal year prior to the award year (September 30, 2007), subtracting this number 135 from the actual foster child adoptions achieved by the state in FY2008 (150) and multiplying the difference (15) by $1,000 for the award amount ($15,000). (The state's "highest ever foster child adoption rate" for FY2009 would be increased to 10%.)

In: Child Welfare: Federal Role in Assistance... ISBN: 978-1-61209-704-6
Editors: M.G. Raposo, D.M. Carroca

Chapter 2

CHILD WELFARE: SOCIAL SECURITY AND SUPPLEMENTAL SECURITY INCOME (SSI) BENEFITS FOR CHILDREN IN FOSTER CARE

Adrienne L. Fernandes, Scott Szymendera and Emilie Stoltzfus

SUMMARY

An estimated 30,000 children receive Supplemental Security Income (S SI) or other Social Security benefits while in foster care. SSI benefits are available under Title XVI of the Social Security Act for certain disabled children from families with low incomes and minimal assets. Social Security benefits may be paid under Title II of the act to the children of workers who have retired, become disabled, or died.

Federal regulations require that in most cases the Social Security Administration (SSA) select and assign a representative payee—an individual, organization, or government entity—that manages SSI and Social Security payments for children, including those in foster care. Nearly all states designated as the representative payee for a foster child use the child's benefits to support the child in foster care. In *Washington State Department of Social and Health Services v. Guardianship Estate of Keffeler* (hereafter *Keffeler*), the Supreme Court held that the process used by the state of Washington to keep the Social Security benefits received as a child's representative payee was not prohibited by the Social Security Act. The Court also concluded that the use of funds for reimbursement for foster care services was consistent with the act's provisions that such funds be spent for the "use and benefit of the beneficiary" and within the regulatory definition of "current maintenance" (i.e., food, clothing, shelter, medical care, and personal comfort items).

Although the *Keffeler* decision supports states' practice of using SSI and other Social Security benefits for reimbursement of foster care, some child advocates assert that by using these benefits to reimburse the cost of foster care, the state agency denies the child beneficiaries funding that rightly belongs to them. Advocates also raise concern that child welfare agencies are often automatically assigned as the representative payee for foster children. On the other hand, child welfare agencies and other advocates argue that if states were not able to use benefits to pay for a child's foster care, they would stop screening children to determine their eligibility for these Social Security programs. They further raise the concern that if a foster child's SSI benefits were allowed to accumulate in a savings account, the child would soon surpass the "means test" for SSI and would lose eligibility for the benefits.

Changes governing how child welfare agencies are assigned as representative payees or how they use the Social Security benefits of foster children would require congressional action. For example, Congress could permit or require states that act as representative payees to "pass through" some or all benefits to eligible foster children and those children could receive a portion of the benefits while in care and/or upon leaving care. Congress could also make changes to the selection of representative payees so that certain individuals, such as the child's attorney, would have the opportunity to serve as the payee.

Legislation introduced in the 110th Congress would have prohibited the use of SSI or Title II Social Security benefits to reimburse a state for foster care maintenance payments, required state child welfare agencies to screen foster children for benefits, and for any foster child already receiving benefits, it would have also required the state to develop a plan to "conserve benefits not necessary for the immediate needs of the child" to enable the child to "achieve self-support after leaving foster care." No legislation regarding this issue has been introduced in the 111th Congress. This report will be updated.

INTRODUCTION

In the past decade, media attention to the case of John G., a North Carolina foster child who received Social Security Survivors benefits, renewed debate concerning the use of foster children's Social Security payments to fund their foster care.[1] John G. was at risk of losing the modest house he inherited from his deceased father if mortgage payments were not made. The county in which he resides was designated by the Social Security Administration to manage his Survivors benefits. Arguing that the benefits should be used to cover the costs of his foster care, the county had declined to use them to make the mortgage payments. However, a county court judge ruled that the county must pay the mortgage and, in November 2007, the Court of Appeals affirmed this ruling.[2]

On any given day, roughly half a million children are in foster care due to incidents of abuse, neglect, or other reasons that prevented them from remaining with their parents. Of these children and youth, an estimated 29,000 received Supplemental Security Income (S SI) under Title XVI of the Social Security Act or another Social Security benefit (e.g., survivor's benefits) under Title II of that act.[3] The Social Security Administration (SSA) may designate a government entity as the representative payee of a foster child if the child's custodial or non-custodial parents, guardians, relatives, stepparents, or a close friend are not available to serve in that role. As the representative payee, the state (like any other representative payee) is required to manage the child's benefits and to use the benefits for the current maintenance (food, clothing, shelter, medical care, and personal comfort items) of the child. Nearly all states use SSI and/or other Social Security benefits to pay for foster care. Among 38 states, including the District of Columbia, that were able to report on their use of these benefits in state FY2006, these benefits totaled $156.6 million.[4]

In recent years, some child welfare advocates have legally challenged the practice of using foster children's SSI and other Social Security benefits to reimburse states for the cost of providing their foster care. The most prominent case, *Washington State Department of Social and Health Services v. Guardianship Estate of Keffeler*, reached the U.S. Supreme Court, which, in 2003, upheld this practice.[5] Nonetheless, the *Keffeler* decision did raise some questions about the federal government's role in regulating the use of Social Security and SSI payments to fund foster care, and some advocates remain concerned about this use of the benefits.

This report begins with a discussion of the foster care system and the Social Security benefits available to eligible children, including those in foster care. It then describes the role of representative payees and their responsibilities. The report provides data on the use of Social Security benefits to reimburse states for child welfare, and includes a discussion of the *Keffeler* decision. Finally, the report concludes with proposals supported by some advocates to change the current practice of using SSI and other Social Security benefits to fund foster care.

Overview of Foster Care

Foster care is the round-the-clock care of a child outside the child's home and is typically necessary because of neglect or physical abuse of the child by his or her parents. Children who are removed from their homes may be placed in foster family homes, institutions, or group homes by the state child welfare agency.

Federal Requirements Applicable to All Foster Care Children

The federal government has established certain requirements related to state provision of foster care that are applicable to all children in foster care. These include that a state has a written case plan detailing, among other things, where the child is placed and what services are to be provided to ensure that a permanent home is re-established for the child. Further, for each child in foster care, this plan must be reviewed on a regular basis, including a review by a judge no less often than every 12 months. For many children who enter foster care, returning to their parents is the way permanence is re-established. For some children, however, it is not safe or possible to reunite with their parents. In those cases states must work to find adoptive parents or legal guardians who can provide a permanent home and family for these children.

Title IV-E Federal Foster Care Program

Title IV-E of the Social Security Act authorizes the federal foster care program.[6] Under this program, a state may seek federal funds for partial reimbursement of the room and board costs needed to support eligible children who are neglected, abused, or who, for some other reason, cannot remain in their own homes. Funding for the Title IV-E foster care program is appropriated out of the general treasury and is available on an open-ended entitlement basis. This means the federal government is obligated to reimburse states for every eligible cost made on behalf of an eligible child.

More than half a million children are in foster care in the United States on any given day of the year and a little less than half of these are estimated to be qualified for federal foster care support under Title IV-E. To be eligible for Title IV-E, a child must (1) meet income/assets tests and family structure rules in the home he/she was removed from;[7] (2) have specific judicial determinations made related to reasons for the removal and other aspects of his/her removal and placement; and (3) be placed in an eligible licensed setting with an eligible provider(s).

Foster Care Maintenance Payment

The state child welfare agency is required to use federal Title IV-E funds to provide a "foster care maintenance payment" to the home or institution where the eligible child is placed to provide for their care and safety. Title IV-E defines a "foster care maintenance payment" as "payments to cover the cost of (and the cost of providing) food, clothing, shelter, daily supervision, school supplies, a child's personal incidentals, liability insurance with respect to a child, reasonable travel to the child's home for visitation and reasonable travel for the child to remain in the school in which the child is enrolled at the time of placement."[8]

States are allowed to determine how much the total foster care maintenance payment will be for each child, and even within states the amounts may vary considerably based on factors like the child's age, special needs, or placement setting (e.g. home vs. institution). The portion of each eligible foster care maintenance payment that is reimbursed by the federal government is determined by the state's Federal Medical Assistance Percentage (FMAP), which may range from 50%, in states with the highest per capita income, to a maximum of 83%, in the lowest per capita states.[9] In FY2008, the most recent year for which these data are available, states made foster care maintenance payments on behalf of an average of 197,200 Title IV-E eligible children each month at a cost of $2.7 billion, and claimed federal reimbursement of $1.5 billion—or roughly 56% of those total maintenance payment costs. For FY2008 then, the total average monthly maintenance payment cost per eligible foster care recipient was a little more than $1,148 and of this amount, the federal government reimbursed states roughly $638.[10]

Use of Child Support

Child Support Enforcement is a federal-state program, authorized under Title IV-D of the Social Security Act, which collects payments from non-custodial parents for the support of their children. In general, child support payments made on behalf of a child who is receiving Title IV-E foster care maintenance payments may be used to reimburse the state and federal governments for the cost of those payments. In FY2008, states collected about $85 million in child support payments made on behalf of children in foster care as reimbursement for Title IV-E foster care maintenance payments. Of this amount, close to $48 million was sent to the federal government to reimburse its share of the foster care maintenance payment costs.[11]

States are required under the Title IV-E foster care program to "where appropriate," take all steps necessary to ensure that the rights to any child support payments of a foster child who receives a Title IV-E foster care maintenance payment are assigned to the state.[12]

Rules for the distribution of any child support collected on behalf of a child eligible for Title IV-E foster care maintenance payments are included in Title IV-D.[13] Any support payments received must first be used to reimburse the state for the cost of a foster care maintenance payment (and a portion of these funds must also be sent to the federal government to reimburse some part of its share of the cost). If the monthly child support payment exceeds the amount needed to reimburse the monthly foster care maintenance payment, then the additional funds are to be paid to the state child welfare agency, which must use the funds "in the manner it determines will serve the best interests of the child."[14] The statute suggests that this might include "setting aside amounts for the child's future needs or making all or part of the amount available to the person responsible for meeting the child's daily needs to be used for the child's benefit." Third, if any amounts collected exceed these first two required distributions, the remaining amount is again to be distributed to the state for reimbursement (to the state and the federal government) of any past foster care maintenance payments (or Temporary Assistance for Needy Families support) received by the child.

Other Reimbursable Costs

In addition to the maintenance payment, the Title IV-E foster care program reimburses other eligible costs that are related to case management and child placement services, and other foster care program administrative costs (so long as they are made on behalf of eligible children). In FY2008, the federal share of these costs, commonly referred to as simply "administrative" costs, was $2.0 billion. States are also permitted to claim some reimbursement for training costs related to provision of foster care (so long as they are made on behalf of eligible children) and for data collection (without regard to whether or not a child is Title IV-E eligible). For FY2007, the federal share of Title IV-E claims for those purposes was about $339 million. Finally, a number of states receive Title IV-E support under special waiver authority that enables them to use the funds for a broader range of child welfare purposes than would otherwise be possible under the Title IV- E foster care program. For FY2008, $640 million in Title IV-E foster care funding was distributed to certain states under child welfare waiver demonstration authority.[15]

Support for Foster Children Not Eligible for Title IV-E

An estimated quarter of a million children in foster care—that is, children removed from their homes and given over to the care and placement responsibility of the state—do not meet the federal Title IV-E eligibility criteria. The federal government does not explicitly require that a state make a foster care maintenance payment on behalf of these children. Practically speaking, however, placing such a child in an out-of-home setting without providing some reimbursement for the cost of that child is difficult, and in many circumstances might be considered a questionable exercise of the state's responsibility for the child. Accordingly all states are believed to provide payments on behalf of children who are placed out of the home and under the responsibility of the state, regardless of the child's Title IV-E eligibility status. (However, some states do pay lesser amounts to relatives who provide foster care for non-Title IV-E eligible children.)[16] In general, maintenance payments to support foster children who are not Title IV-E eligible must be supplied by the state (or local) government.[17] States may also seek child support payments on behalf of foster children who are not Title IV-E eligible and may use these funds to reimburse the cost of providing foster care to the child.

To offset the administrative costs (costs related to case management and child placement services, training, data collection and other administrative costs) of providing foster care to children not eligible under Title IV-E, states may use federal funding provided under the Title IV-B programs (all of the Stephanie Tubbs Jones Child Welfare Services funding, and some of the

Promoting Safe and Stable Families funds, combined FY20 10 federal funding of $690 million). However, these children are largely supported in care with non-federal (state or local) dollars, as well as some dollars from federal funding streams not solely dedicated to child welfare purposes. These include the Temporary Assistance to Needy Families (TANF) block grant, the Social Services Block Grant (SSBG), and Medicaid. [18]

Youth Who "Age Out" of Foster Care

Despite the effort to find a permanent home for all foster children, some children reach the age of majority (18 years of age in most states) and thus "age-out" of foster care before a new permanent home is found for them. An estimated 29,500 children "aged-out" of foster care during FY2008.[19] In general, federal Title IV-E funding is available for foster care youth until their 18th birthday.[20] However, beginning with FY20 11, states have the option to seek federal reimbursement for the cost of providing foster care to eligible youth until age 19, 20, or 21—whichever age the state selects.[21] The youth must meet certain criteria to stay in care. They must be completing high school or a program leading to an equivalent credential; enrolled in an institution that provides post-secondary or vocational education; participating in a program or activity designed to promote, or remove barriers to, employment; or employed at least 80 hours per month (i.e., part- time). States may also seek reimbursement for an older youth's foster care if the youth has a medical condition that makes him or her incapable of participating in the activity, and this incapacity is supported by regularly updated information in the youth's case plan. States that wish to extend care must still provide services to help foster youth make the transition to independent adulthood, and they currently receive some funds (through the Chafee Foster Care Independence Program and a related Education and Training Vouchers program, combined FY20 10 funding of roughly $185 million) to continue certain independent living services to youth after they leave foster care.[22]

Separately, states are required to provide services to help foster youth make the transition to independent adulthood and are provided some funds (through the Chafee Foster Care Independence Program and a related Education and Training Vouchers program, combined

FY20 10 funding of roughly $185 million) to continue certain independent living services to youth after they leave foster care.[23] With one exception, these funds may not be used for services or activities that assist youth once they have reached their 21st birthday and states are limited in the amount of these funds that may be spent for room and board costs.[24]

Social Security and Supplemental Security Income (SSI) Benefits for Children

Titles II and XVI of the Social Security Act provide two types of benefits for children, including those in foster care, who meet certain qualifications. Social Security benefits (formally called Old-Age, Survivors, and Disability Insurance benefits) are authorized under Title II of the act. Social Security benefits may be paid to the children of workers who have retired, become disabled, or died.[25] These benefits are paid out of the Social Security Trust Funds. SSI benefits are authorized under Title XVI of the act. SSI benefits are available for certain children with disabilities if their families have low incomes and minimal assets. SSI benefits are paid out of general revenues.[26] Most states supplement the monthly SSI benefit with state or territorial funds.

Table 1 shows the number of children who receive SSI and other Social Security benefits, as well as the total amount of monthly federal and state supplementary benefits paid to these children.

Table 1. All Children Receiving Social Security and SSI Benefits, December 2009

Program	Number of Children (under age 18)	Total Amount of Monthly Benefits *($; includes federal benefits and state supplements)*
Social Security[a]	3,158,138	1,592,355,462
Supplemental Security Income (SSI)	1,204,089	749,310,00

Source: The Congressional Research Service (CRS). Data on Social Security benefits taken from the website of the Social Security Administration, Office of the Chief Actuary at http://www.ssa.gov/OACT/ProgData/ benefits.html. Data on SSI benefits taken from Social Security Administration, SSI Monthly Statistics, December 2009, Washington, DC, January 2010, Tables 2 and 6.

Note: Numbers may be rounded.

a. Includes children of retired, deceased, or disabled workers only.

Social Security Benefits for Children (Title II)

A child may be eligible for Social Security benefits if he or she is the biological child, adopted child, or dependent stepchild of a person eligible for certain Social Security benefits. In some cases, dependent grandchildren of persons eligible for Social Security benefits may also be eligible for benefits. In order to qualify for benefits, the child must be unmarried and have a parent that meets one of the following conditions:

- the parent is disabled or retired and is entitled to either Social Security old age (i.e., retirement) or disability benefits; or
- the parent is deceased and was fully insured for Social Security benefits based on work history at the time of death.

Social Security benefits for children are intended to replace the household income lost due to retirement, disability, or death that might otherwise have been spent to provide for dependent children unable to care for themselves or earn their own money through work.

Benefit Amounts for Children

Children who qualify for Social Security benefits may receive up to 50% of a living parent's full retirement or disability benefit or 75% of the deceased parent's Social Security benefit. Benefits for children are subject to the family maximum rules which limit the total amount of benefits available to any one family to between 150% and 180% of the parent's full benefit amount. If the total amount of all family benefits exceeds this maximum amount, then the benefit of each person, except the parent, is reduced proportionately.

When Children's Benefits Stop

An eligible child may receive Social Security benefits until the child reaches the age of 18, or 19 if the child is still in high school. Benefits may continue during adulthood if the child has a disability that began before he or she turned 22. Children's benefits terminate upon the marriage of the child at any age.

SSI Benefits for Children (Title XVI)

A child who is blind or has a severe disability may be eligible to receive SSI benefits regardless of the work history or benefit status of his or her parents.[27] In order to qualify for SSI benefits, the child must meet the statutory definition of blindness or disability, and the income and resources of the family must fall below limits set in Title XVI of the act.

A child is considered blind for the purposes of SSI eligibility if the child has central visual acuity of 20/200 or less in his or her better eye with the use of a correcting lens. A child is considered disabled for the purposes of SSI eligibility if that child meets each of the following three conditions:

- the child must have a physical or mental impairment that results in "marked and severe functional limitations";[28]
- the child must have a condition that has lasted or is expected to last at least 12 months or result in death; and
- the child must either earn less than the substantial gainful activity amount ($1,000 per month for 2010) or not work.

SSI benefits are designed to provide a minimum level of monthly income to disabled persons and families with disabled children who have limited means and limited other options for financial assistance. A child must fall below the income and resources limits established by the SSI program. Since children rarely have income or resources of their own, the Social Security Administration (SSA) uses a process called "deeming" to assign part of the value of the income and resources of the parents to disabled children for the purposes of determining SSI eligibility. In order to qualify for SSI benefits, a child's countable deemed income and assets must fall below program guidelines.[29] Children living in foster care do not have the income of the family they are living with deemed to them and this income is not counted against them when determining SSI eligibility. SSI income limits vary by state and type of income.

Once a child in the SSI program reaches age 18, his or her case is reviewed by SSA to determine if he or she meets the SSI disability standard for adults, which is based on an inability to perform work rather than functional limitations. At age 18, the income and resources of parents are no longer considered available (i.e., deemed) to a child.

SSI Asset Limits and Assets Not Counted As Resources in the SSI Program

The countable resource limit for SSI eligibility is $2,000 for individuals and $3,000 for couples. These limits are set by law, are not indexed for inflation, and have been at their current levels since 1989.[30] In most cases, the resources of the family that a child lives with are counted as the child's resources when determining his or her SSI eligibility. However, children living in foster care are considered to be living on their own and the resources and income of the household they are living in are not considered when determining their SSI eligibility. Not all resources are counted for the purposes of determining SSI eligibility. The Social Security Act and federal regulations provide various types of resource exclusions that allow individuals or couples to own certain assets and not have them counted against their $2,000 or $3,000 resource limit.[31]

The SSI resource rules make it difficult for beneficiaries to accumulate assets while receiving benefits. Children who receive SSI benefits cannot build up savings for use during adulthood or to pay for post-secondary education expenses without jeopardizing their eligibility for SSI benefits. Like other children who receive SSI benefits, foster children beneficiaries cannot retain eligibility for those benefits if they build up a pool of money in excess of $2,000 to assist in their transition into adulthood and independent living.[32]

Dedicated Accounts for Children

When a child SSI beneficiary is owed back SSI benefits of more than six months, his or her representative payee, discussed below, is required to place those benefits in a dedicated account at a financial institution.[33] The representative payee may use the money from the dedicated account for the medical care; education and training needs of the child; personal needs assistance, special equipment, and housing modifications; or therapy for the child based on his or her disability.[34] Money from a dedicated account cannot be used for the daily expenses, food, clothing, or shelter of the child. Money in a dedicated account for children is not counted as a resource for the purposes of determining the child's SSI eligibility.

Representative Payees in the Social Security System

Although most Social Security and SSI payments are made directly from SSA to the beneficiary, the Social Security Act allows the agency to make payments to a representative payee acting on the beneficiary's behalf. This representative payee may be an individual, organization, or a state/local agency working on behalf of the beneficiary and must meet strict guidelines established in the act.[35] Individuals acting as representative payees may not charge a fee for their services. However, organizations serving in this capacity can charge a small fee to cover administrative costs associated with handling payments.

Over 7.8 million Social Security and SSI beneficiaries receive payments through representative payees each month. The use of representative payees is more prevalent in the SSI program as 37% of SSI beneficiaries have a representative payee while only 10% of Social Security beneficiaries receive their benefits through a representative payee. [36]

Representative Payees for Children Receiving Benefits

Federal regulations state that in most cases SSA will assign a representative payee for children who receive Social Security or SSI benefits.[37] Exceptions may be made and payments may be given directly to the child if he or she is nearing age 18, serving in the military, supporting himself or herself, or is a parent. In addition, children under 18 who receive Social Security disability benefits because of their own work history and disability may receive benefits without a representative payee.

Order of Selection of Representative Payees

It is the responsibility of SSA to select the person or organization who will serve as a representative payee. The regulations provide for an order of selection to guide the agency in selecting a payee.[38] The order of selection is just a guide and in all cases the best interests of the beneficiary are to be considered when assigning a representative payee. The order of selection for children receiving benefits:

- First: A natural or adoptive parent who has custody, or a legal guardian.
- Second: A natural or adoptive parent who does not have custody, but who is contributing to the support of the child and is demonstrating a strong concern for the well being of the child.

- Third: A natural or adoptive parent who does not have custody, and who is not contributing to the support of the child but is demonstrating a strong concern for the well being of the child.
- Fourth: A relative or stepparent who has custody of the child.
- Fifth: A relative or stepparent who does not have custody, but who is contributing to the support of the child and is demonstrating a strong concern for the well being of the child.
- Sixth: A relative or close friend of the child who does not have custody but is demonstrating concern for the well being of the child.
- Seventh: An authorized social services agency or custodial institution.

As shown in **Table 2,** a child's natural or adoptive parents act as representative payees in nearly 82% of SSI cases. Grandparents and other relatives act as payees for children in nearly 14% of cases while social service agencies act as representative payees for children in the SSI program in 2% of cases.

Table 2. Types of Representative Payees for Children in the SSI Program, December 2008

Type of Payee	Number of SSI Children	Percent of All SSI Children
No payee	1,000	0.1
Natural or adoptive parents	944,112	81.9
Spouse	32	0.0
Natural, adoptive, or stepchild	451	0.0
Grandparent	76,288	6.6
Other relative	85,035	7.4
Non-mental institution	6,303	0.5
Mental institution	2,359	0.2
Financial organization	200	0.0
Social services agency	18,375	1.6
Public official	1,339	0.1
Other	18,350	1.6
Total	**1,152,844**	**100.0**

Source: Table prepared by Congressional Research Service (CRS) based on Social Security Administration, *SSI Annual Statistical Report, 2008*, Washington, DC, September 2009, Table 7.

Note: Numbers may not add up due to rounding. The SSA does not define each type of representative payee.

The SSA's Program Operations Manual System (POMS), which provides internal guidance for SSA employees, specifies that when a social service agency is awarded custody of a child who is removed from the custody of a parent, the agency retains custody regardless of whether the child is placed in a foster home or group living household.[39] The POMS advises that the social service agency should not be routinely appointed as representative payee, and that SSA employees should consider a number of factors in assigning a payee:

- how the social services agency became responsible for the child;
- whether the child is expected to return to the custody of a parent, and if so, when;
- the source of the child's support;
- who has physical custody of the child;
- the nature and extent of the child welfare agency's care;
- whether the agency has temporary or permanent custody;
- whether parental rights have been terminated; and
- whether there are concerned relatives and friends.

Responsibilities of Representative Payees

The responsibilities of child welfare agencies serving as representative payees for child beneficiaries are the same as those of other types of payees. The representative payees' major statutory and regulatory obligations involve how the beneficiaries' benefits are managed.

Statutory Responsibilities

Sections 205(j)(1)(A) and 1632(a)(2)(A)(I) of the act specify that SSA may assign a representative payee to a beneficiary if the agency determines the "interest of the individual" beneficiary would be served by such an assignment. The act further specifies that the payment to the representative payee must be used for the "use and benefit" of the beneficiary.[40]

Regulatory Responsibilities

Federal regulations require that a representative payee "use the payments he or she receives only for the use and benefit of the beneficiary in a manner and for the purposes he or she determines ... to be in the best interests of the beneficiary."[41] The regulations then define the concept of "use and benefit of the beneficiary" by stating:

> We will consider that payments we certify to a representative payee have been used for the use and benefit of the beneficiary if they are used for the beneficiary's current maintenance. Current maintenance includes costs incurred in obtaining food, shelter, clothing, medical care, and personal comfort items.[42]

Special Rules Concerning Creditors and Debts

Sections 205(j)(2)(C)(i)(III) and 1631 (a)(2)(B)(iii)(III) of the act prohibit creditors who provide goods and services to the beneficiary from serving as that beneficiary's representative payee.[43] However, Sections 205(j)(2)(C)(iii)(III) and 1631 (a)(2)(B)(v)(III) of the act make an exception to this provision if the creditor is "a facility that is licensed or certified as a care facility under the law of a State or a political subdivision of a State."[44]

The regulations also include rules regarding the payment of debts to creditors and specify that "A payee may not be required to use benefit payments to satisfy a debt of the beneficiary, if the debt arose prior to the first month for which payments are certified to a payee. If the debt arose prior to this time, a payee may satisfy it only if the current and reasonably foreseeable needs of the beneficiary are met."[45]

Children in Foster Care Receiving or Potentially Eligible for SSI

In December 2008, 1.2 million children, or 1.6% of the total child population in the United States, received SSI.[46] To be eligible for SSI, a child must have a physical or mental impairment that results in "marked and severe functional limitations," the limitations are expected to last at least 12 months or result in death, and the child's family is low income and has minimal assets. Just under two-thirds of all children who received an SSI benefit were diagnosed with a "mental disorder" (51.6% with an "other" mental disorder and 14.1% with "mental retardation").[47] Nearly all of the remaining recipients were diagnosed with serious health conditions, such as a disorder of the nervous system and sense organs or congenital abnormalities, among other conditions.

Compared to children in the general population, children in foster care have greater physical and mental health and developmental needs. Researchers studying a nationally representative sample of children placed in out of home care (following an investigation for child abuse or neglect) estimated that more than 20% had physical or mental health conditions that—given the severity of the condition and the length of the condition or risk of death—would likely make them eligible for SSI. Among children who had been in out of home care for at least one year this percentage rose slightly to 21%. The researchers based these findings on direct assessments of children and standardized questionnaires administered to caregivers about the child's social skills, behavior, or health status. Slightly more than half of the children in out of home care the researchers assumed would be eligible (i.e., the 20% that had the physical or mental health condition), scored significantly lower than the mean across these domains. Because of the survey methodology, the researchers deemed their estimate of SSI eligibility among children in out of home care as "modest," however, it is considerably higher then the estimated 5% to 7% of children in foster care who are reported as receiving SSI (or other Social Security benefits).[48]

The study also compared eligibility for SSI across age, race and ethnicity, locality, and gender. Of the sample of children in out of home care, the estimated rate of SSI eligibility was significantly higher among those ages 6 through 10 (compared to children younger than age 6 and older than age 10) and those in rural settings (compared to urban settings), but there was no significant differences on the basis of race, ethnicity, or gender. Among children who were in care for at least one year, age was not a significant factor in predicting possible SSI eligibility; however, a much greater share of black children (compared to white children) and boys would likely qualify, and a slightly higher share of children in urban settings would likely qualify.

Given their health and mental health needs—and the fact that most foster children would be expected to meet the income and resources requirements for SSI receipt—it is possible that at least some foster children who would be eligible for SSI are not receiving benefits. This may be attributable to two factors. First, not all children in foster care may have been screened for SSI eligibility. Among the 25 states that responded to a 2006 American Public Human Services Association (APHSA) survey of state child welfare agencies regarding their SSI screening practices, 18 reported "routinely" screening foster children for SSI eligibility while the remaining seven indicated that screening might be done but was not routine.[49] An agency may also decide not to pursue SSI eligibility for a given foster child, if the agency determines receipt of a Title IV-E federal foster care benefit better serves the child. On the other hand, SSI eligibility, once determined, may be maintained into adulthood (with re-determinations) where eligibility for a foster care maintenance payment ceases generally at, or soon after, a youth's 18th birthday.

Concurrent Receipt of Benefits

The *Child Welfare Policy Manual*, which discusses official guidance (including law, regulations, and policies) on the Title IV-E foster care program, states that there is no prohibition against claiming both an SSI benefit and a Title IV-E supported foster care maintenance payment.[50] However, the policy manual notes that the amount of the foster care maintenance payment received will reduce a child's SSI benefit, dollar for dollar. Thus if a child's total monthly foster care maintenance payment is $500—and that maintenance payment is in part paid with federal Title IV-E dollars—then the child's SSI benefit would be reduced by $500.[51]

For children in foster care who do not qualify for Title IV-E foster care support, states must find other sources of funding to pay for that child. Most non-Title IV-E eligible children in foster care must be supported with state or local dollars. Such payments generally do not reduce an SSIeligible foster child's federal SSI benefit because they are not counted as income.[52] Typically, however, a state, acting as the child's representative payee, is believed to use SSI or Social Security benefits to provide a foster care maintenance payment to the child (or to reimburse itself for that payment).

Addressing the question about whether to apply for either or both Title IV-E and SSI benefits, the *Child Welfare Policy Manual* counsels careful review of benefits available under each program "so that an informed choice can be made in the child's best interest." It adds that "to achieve this goal, title IV-E agencies should exchange information regarding eligibility requirements and benefits with local Social Security district offices and establish formal procedures to refer clients and their representative to the local Social Security district office for consultation and/or application when appropriate."[53] The dollar value of the respective benefit is often a consideration.[54] At the same time, even if the interaction of Title IV-E and SSI payments appears to negate the benefit of applying for SSI, establishing SSI eligibility for a child for a child whose permanency plan is to reunite with his or her parents may help those parents (or other family members) better meet the child's needs when this goal is reached.

The eligibility for and amount of Title II benefits are not affected by receipt of foster care. Social Security benefits are paid under Title II to the children of workers who have retired, become disabled, or died. Their eligibility is determined by their parents' participation in the workforce. Because both SSI and Title IV-E foster care have income- and resources-related eligibility criteria, children who are recipients of Title II Social Security benefits may be less likely to qualify for either of the means-tested programs.

Use of SSI and Other Social Security Benefits by Child Welfare Agencies

Most, if not all, states use Social Security and/or SSI benefits of children in foster care as a source of federal funds for their foster care programs. Exactly how much child welfare funding is derived from these benefits is uncertain. The recent Casey Child Welfare Financing Survey, conducted by Child Trends, found that for state fiscal year (SFY) 2006, 37 states and the District of Columbia were able to provide some data on the amount of SSI and Title II benefits (including Survivor's and Social Security Disability (SSDI) benefits)[55] used by the state child welfare agency.[56] These states represented roughly 61% of the FY2006 foster care caseload.[57]

Among the states that provided data to Child Trends, Social Security benefits (SSI and Title II) made up $156.6 million in funding for child welfare. **Table 3** shows the reported data by the reporting states. (Assuming all states spent these funds at roughly the same rate as those that reported data, total use of Social Security benefits by state child welfare agencies would be roughly $258 million.[58])

Although not insignificant, spending of Social Security benefits on child welfare represents a relatively small share of the $25.7 billion in total spending reported by child welfare agencies for SFY2006 (roughly half of these expended funds, $12.4 billion, were federal dollars). On average, among the state child welfare agencies that reported data on the use of Social Security benefits, these benefits represented 1.26% of the federal dollars spent and less than 1% (0.61%) of their total spending.

Table 3. Social Security (SSI and Title II) Benefits as Funding Stream for Child Welfare Spending, SFY2006

State	Social Security Spending ($)	Benefits Used as Share of State Child Welfare Agencies—	
		Total Spending (%)	Federal Spending (%)
Alabama	$5,500,000	1.84	3.33
Alaska	818,500	0.76	1.78
Arizona	890,000	0.20	0.35
Arkansas	2,661,478	2.60	4.25
Colorado	5,157,020	1.14	2.32
Connecticut	906,137	0.13	0.23
District of Columbia	750,000	0.28	0.75
Delaware	408,880	0.77	3.33
Florida	10,146,518	1.01	2.03
Hawaii	262,777	0.23	0.49
Illinois	18,733,102	1.51	3.11
Iowa	3,627,848	1.04	1.91
Kansas	3,572,042	1.24	4.64
Kentucky	6,768,992	1.64	4.03
Louisiana	3,093,027	1.39	2.34
Maine	1,808,278	1.49	4.89
Massachusetts	6,687,044	0.93	2.60
Michigan	7,504,132	0.90	1.50
Missouri	7,462,631	1.81	3.35
Montana	2,000,000	3.24	6.43
Nebraska	3,997,857	2.17	4.32
Nevada	627,587	0.62	1.15
New Hampshire	1,245,869	1.53	2.58
New Jersey	1,490,000	0.21	0.59
New Mexico	1,584,061	2.17[a]	2.90[a]
Oklahoma	4,487,425	1.81	3.26
Oregon	4,997,717	1.22	1.97
Pennsylvania	13,737,700	0.85	3.53

Table 3. (Continued)

State	Social Security Spending ($)	Benefits Used as Share of State Child Welfare Agencies—	
		Total Spending (%)	Federal Spending (%)
Rhode Island	1,857,103	0.89	2.14
South Dakota	773,042	1.37	2.45
Tennessee	5,178,585	0.99	2.19
Texas	9,962,658	0.98a	1.53a
Utah	768,271	0.56	1.24
Vermont	1,376,948	1.58	2.71
Washington	10,591,342	2.20	4.53
West Virginia	1,872,703	1.01	2.14
Wisconsin	3,037,596	0.92	1.79
Wyoming	288,679	1.07	2.60
Total	**156,633,548**	**0.61**	**1.26**

Source: Congressional Research Service (CRS) table based on revised data provided by Child Trends from the Casey Child Welfare Financing Survey, which examined state child welfare agency spending for SFY2006.

Note: The following 13 states indicated that data on the use of Social Security benefits were unavailable: California, Georgia, Idaho, Indiana, Maryland, Minnesota, Mississippi, New York, North Carolina, North Dakota, Ohio, South Carolina, and Virginia.

a. New Mexico and Texas reported child support dollars in their response for Social Security benefits. These dollars are included as part of the total calculation, as reported by Child Trends.

KEFFELER DECISION

In recent years, some child welfare advocates have legally challenged states' practice of using foster children's SSI and Title II benefits to reimburse the cost of providing foster care to those children. The most prominent case, *Washington State Department of Social and Health Services v. Guardianship Estate of Keffeler*, reached the U.S. Supreme Court in 2002. The Supreme Court ruled unanimously (in 2003) that the state of Washington could, as the representative payee for a foster child receiving Social Security or SSI benefits, use the child's benefits to reimburse itself for the cost of that child's foster care.[59] This case reached the U.S. Supreme Court on the appeal of the state of Washington, which was seeking to overturn the previous ruling of the Washington State Supreme Court (discussed below).

The Decision of the Washington State Supreme Court

In 2001, the Washington State Supreme Court ruled in *Guardianship Estate of Danny Keffeler v. Department of Social and Health Services* that the state of Washington's service as a representative payee for children in foster care violated the anti-attachment clause of the Social Security Act.[60] In its decision, the Washington State Supreme Court stated that "the facial logic of DSHS 's reimbursement scheme demonstrates a creditor relationship, a relationship involving creditor-type acts, vis-á-vis foster children and their SSA benefits." The Washington State Supreme Court also cited, among other cases, the decision of the Ninth Circuit in *Brinkman v. Rahm* that prohibited the state of Washington from deducting Social Security payments as reimbursement for the costs associated with the care of persons with mental illnesses involuntarily confined to state hospitals.[61]

While the Washington State Supreme Court did not directly rule on whether the actions of the Washington Department of Social and Health Services as a representative payee violated other sections of the Social Security Act, it did discuss whether the state was acting in the best interest of the child entitled to benefits. The Washington State Supreme Court stated that a child in foster care is "better off with any payee other than the state because the state must provide foster care under state law regardless of whether it receives reimbursement" and that "we seriously doubt using the SSA benefits to reimburse the state for its public assistance expenditure is in all cases, or even some, 'in the best interests of the beneficiary.'"

The Opinion of the Supreme Court

Justice Souter wrote the unanimous opinion of the Court, which sided with the Washington State Department of Social and Health Services and overturned the decision of the Washington Supreme Court. The U.S. Supreme Court stated that the state could not be a foster child's creditor since the foster child did not have an obligation to pay for his or her foster care.[62] Instead, the question raised by the case, the Court stated was "whether the department's efforts to become a representative payee, or its use of respondents' Social Security benefits when it acts in that capacity amounts to employing an 'execution, levy, attachment, garnishment or other legal process'," to gain control of the children's Social Security benefits.[63] On the question of this alleged violation of what is commonly called the"anti-attachment clause"—the Court held that neither the process used by Washington state to become a representative payee for children in foster care who were recipients of SSI or Social Security benefits, nor its use of those benefits to reimburse the cost of their foster care, violated the anti-attachment clause.[64] The Court further noted that the use of funds to reimburse the Washington State Department of Social and Health Services for foster care was consistent with the regulatory requirement that such funds be spent for the "use and benefit of the beneficiary" and with the regulatory definition of "current maintenance" that includes "costs incurred in obtaining food, shelter, clothing, medical care, and personal comfort items."[65]

The U.S. Supreme Court further asserted that the "real basis" of the respondent's objection in the case (and the previous Washington State Supreme Court's holding in the case) was the "view that allowing a state agency to reimburse itself for the costs of foster care is antithetical to the best interest of the beneficiary foster child."[66] Responding to this issue, the Court first relied on the settled principle of administrative law that an open-ended and potentially vague term, such as "best interest" is "highly susceptible to administrative interpretation subject to judicial deference."[67] Thus, it noted that SSA has the authority to determine, through regulation, how it will interpret this part of the law. The Court then concluded that SSA's regulations on this issue are consistent with the basic objectives of the law authorizing the SSI and Social Security programs. Specifically, those are to provide a minimum level of income, and the basic objective of the Social Security program is to provide income required for ordinary and necessary living expenses.[68] The Social Security Commissioner, the Court wrote, "has decided that a representative payee serves the beneficiary's interest by seeing that basic needs are met, not by maximizing a trust fund attributable to fortuitously overlapping state and federal grants."[69]

Should SSI and Other Social Security Benefits Be Used to Pay for Foster Care?

The *Keffeler* decision affirmed the right of states (under current law) to both act as representative payees for children in foster care who are recipients of federal Social Security and SSI benefits and further to use those benefits to reimburse the cost of foster care. State child welfare agencies and many child welfare advocates applauded the decision; other advocates remain concerned that the practice of states using foster children's SSI or Social Security benefits to pay for foster care does not serve these children's best interests.[70]

Benefits Should Not be Used for Foster Care

Some legal advocates argue that the state agency is more interested in gaining federal funds than it is in ensuring that a child's benefits serve his/her best interests, and that a child's benefits are not necessarily used to benefit just the child but may simply defray child welfare or foster care expenses for the state generally.[71] Further, they argue that even the practice of applying the benefits solely for the beneficiaries' foster care costs amounts to asking children to pay for their own stay in foster care, while other children in care (including those with assets or income other than Social Security or those who receive Social Security benefits but have a representative payee other than the child welfare agency) are not required to repay the costs.[72] Additionally some advocates are concerned that child welfare agencies may be automatically assigned as the representative payee for children in foster care, even though (under SSA's own regulations) the agencies should be the least preferred representative payee. Related to this concern, some advocates suggest that SSA does not perform adequate investigations to determine whether a more suitable payee is available.[73] Further, according to some legal advocates, agencies that receive a poor review by SSA or fail to submit payee accounting reports to SSA continue to serve as payees.[74]

Rather than paying for a child's foster care, these advocates argue that any SSI and other Social Security benefits that a child is eligible to receive should be invested or otherwise saved for the child's future use (e.g., education, housing). Youth who leave foster care without a permanent home, typically at age 18, often have a difficult time securing housing and income sufficient to shelter and support themselves. S SI-eligible foster care youth who exit foster care would arguably have an even more difficult time and thus may need additional resources that SSI provides (albeit some youth may continue to be eligible for SSI at age 18 and beyond).[75] Providing benefits to eligible youth upon leaving care could ease the transition to adulthood for these youth at a time when they are expected to become financially independent.

Benefits Should Be Used for Foster Care

State child welfare agencies and many child welfare advocates, however, assert that SSI and Title II funds are critical for child welfare agencies operating on tight budgets and that use these benefits to pay for the cost of current maintenance, is consistent with the federal purpose for providing those funds. (Further, the use of these child-specific funds to reimburse foster care costs is consistent with federal policy for use of child support paid on behalf of the child by the non-custodial parent(s).) Some child welfare advocates argue that states have expended benefits for allowable purposes in good faith, just as a parent serving as a representative payee would. Thus, states should not be held to a different standard than parents or other representative payees.[76] In addition, state child welfare agencies and advocates argue that returning benefits to children that were already used to pay for their maintenance could cost states up to hundreds of millions of dollars.[77] In *Keffeler*, the Supreme Court cited the Amici Curiae briefs filed by the Children's Defense Fund (along with Catholic Charities USA, the Child Welfare League of America, and the Alliance for Children and Families), the State of Florida (along with 38 additional states, Puerto Rico and the territories of American Samoa and the Virgin Islands), and the United States which claimed that without the ability to use Social Security and SSI benefits to reimburse the costs of foster care, states would be discouraged from serving as representative payees because of the administrative costs involved.[78]

Some child welfare advocates express the concern that if states were not able to use SSI or Title II benefits to pay for a child's foster care room and board, then states would simply stop screening children to determine their eligibility for these programs. Screenings by child welfare staff can help to determine an individual child's needs and to secure extra benefits and services not normally available in foster care, such as housing modifications.[79] Eliminating these screenings would do a disservice to potentially qualified children, these advocates argue, because a child's eligibility for SSI or another Title II Social Security benefit may extend beyond his/her stay in foster care, and the benefit could provide crucial support for the child outside the system. (For instance, the benefit could offset the cost of therapeutic care to the families of children who leave care due to adoption or reunification.)[80] The *Keffeler* Court relied on this argument in its decision, asserting that absent this state assistance, "many eligible children would either obtain no Social Security benefits, or need some very good luck to get them."[81]

In addition, these advocates argue that if child SSI beneficiaries were given all of their benefits while in foster care, they might accumulate assets in the form of savings and could soon find themselves above the maximum SSI resource level of $2,000.[82] This might also be the case if another type of representative payee preserved some of the child's benefits for non-maintenance expenses (not paid for out of a dedicated account), including the future costs associated with the transition to adulthood (i.e., rent deposit, vocational training, educational expenses, etc.).

POSSIBLE LEGISLATIVE CHANGES

The decision of the Supreme Court in 2003 upholds states' use of SSI and Social Security benefits for reimbursement of current maintenance for children in foster care. Federally enforceable changes to this practice would require congressional action.[83]

Policy changes might include passing through some of the SSI or Title II benefits to foster children who receive such benefits, making best effort attempts to find alternative representative payees, and increasing the asset limit for youth who receive SSI.

Pass Through Benefits

Congress could permit or require states that act as representative payees to "pass through" some or all of the SSI and Title II benefits to eligible foster children and those children could receive a portion of the benefits while in care and/or upon leaving care. Such a proposal might include a maximum amount of money available to eligible youth. For example, a maximum level could be established at $2,000 because children receiving SSI are not permitted under current law to accumulate more than that amount. Legislation passed by California in 2005 (A.B. 1633) requires the state to consider the feasibility and cost-effectiveness of reserving an amount up to $2,000 to assist youth as they "age out" of foster care.[84] A bill in the 110th Congress, the Foster Care Self- Support Act (H.R. 1104) would have required the state child welfare agency (again as a condition of federal foster care funding) to develop a plan specific to the needs of that child, and that would "conserve benefits not necessary for the immediate needs of the child" to enable the child to "achieve self-support after leaving foster care." Any savings accumulated under the plan would not have been counted for purposes of determining the child's SSI eligibility. The plan would have needed to be developed and implemented in collaboration with the child (on an age- appropriate basis), and the child's social worker, representative payee, and attorney/guardian ad litem.

The Temporary Assistance for Needy Families (TANF) program provides an example of how federal legislation could make more Social Security and SSI benefits available to beneficiaries in foster care.[85] Under current law, as amended by the Child Support Provision of the Deficit Reduction Act of 2005 (P.L. 109-171), families that participate in TANF must assign their child support rights to the state. Child support payments collected by the state (from non-custodial parents) on behalf of these TANF families are used by the state and federal governments as partial reimbursement for the welfare benefits that are provided to the family in much the same way as Social Security and SSI benefits are used to reimburse state governments for child welfare spending.[86] With respect to TANF families, states may choose to pass through some of their share of child support payments collected on behalf of the families (up to $100 per family per month or $200 per month if the family has two or more children) to the family. Currently, 24 states provide some sort of *pass through* of child support payments for families receiving TANF.[87] This type of federal initiative, used for Social Security and SSI benefits, could result in children in foster care receiving part of those benefits instead of the benefits being kept by the states as reimbursement for foster care expenses. However, such a program would result in costs to the states.

Best Efforts to Find Alternative Representative Payees

Some child advocates have proposed changes to the selection of representative payees because of the perceived automatic process by which child welfare agencies are named as the payees for foster care children. First, they suggest that the current practice of providing advance notice in the selection of a representative payee for a child should be clarified because improved notice can assist SSA's efforts to name a payee other than the state.[88] Social Security regulations currently do not list the child or the child's attorney or *guardian ad litem* (an attorney appointed by the judge on behalf of the child) as recipients of the advance notice. According to advocates, the notice should be sent to individual(s) who represent the child in judicial proceedings, as well as the child's parents, current and past foster care or relative caretakers, other parties in the juvenile proceedings, and the juvenile court judge.[89] (As discussed above, H.R. 1104 would require SSA to send this notice to a foster child's attorney or guardian ad litem.)

Second, advocates argue that alternative payees not listed in the SSA preference list[90] should be considered as possible payees. These alternative payees include volunteer representative payee programs developed by non-profit organizations and local government agencies for adult beneficiaries requiring the service.[91] Court Appointed Special Advocates (CASA) could also serve as payees.[92] CASA volunteers are sworn in by local court systems to provide advocacy services on behalf of abused and neglected children. These volunteers may be in the optimal position to report to the court the child's needs because they advocate for the child regardless of changes in their placement goal (i.e., family preservation, family reunification, or adoption) or where the child is placed (i.e., kin and/or foster families). California's 2005 law (AB 1633) requires counties to apply to become the representative payee if no other appropriate party is available to serve while the child is in foster care, although "appropriate party" includes only those individuals currently permitted by SSA. Similarly, the Foster Children Self-Support Act (H.R. 1104) from the 110th Congress would have required states to apply to become the foster child's representative payee "if there is no other suitable candidate available." Although the California law does not provide any further requirement to the counties or the state about the procedures for notifying interested parties about the representative payee selection process, H.R. 1104 would have required notification to a foster child's attorney or guardian ad litem.

Proposals to expand the list of representative payees or to provide advance notice of selecting a representative payee to additional parties may burden SSA. Auditing individuals or non-profit organizations that serve as representative payees—rather than a large organization such as a state child welfare agency—could also strain the administrative capacity of the agency.

Change Asset Levels

Individuals who receive SSI may not accumulate more than $2,000 in resources. This resource limit level has been fixed since 1989, and is not indexed for inflation.[93] Some child advocates argue that increasing the asset level for children receiving SSI would aid those youth as they left foster care.[94] As proposed, H.R. 1104 would exempt assets accumulated by a foster child (under an approved plan) from the SSI eligibility determination.

Changes to the asset limit for certain children in the child welfare system would not be new. The Chafee Foster Care Independence Act (P.L. 106-169) increased the asset limit for children eligible to receive Title IV-E foster care maintenance payments. As discussed previously, eligibility for these payments is based on whether the children's original families would qualify for AFDC, as it was in effect on July 16, 1996. Under those rules, children—before the amendment by P.L. 106- 169—could not remain eligible for Title IV-E services if they accumulated assets of more than $1,000. In its report recommending this change the House Ways and Means Committee noted:

> Children in foster care have a special need for resources. Unlike children reared in families, these children often have little or no support from relatives. Thus, when they turn age 18 and are no longer eligible for government foster care payments, they are on their own. Under current law, these adolescents cannot accumulate more than $1,000 in assets and still remain eligible for Federal foster care payments. The Committee believes children in foster care should be allowed to accumulate a much higher level of assets to prepare for the day when they must support themselves. Thus, we are increasing the asset limit to $10,000.[95]

By contrast, under the SSI program, individuals are generally no longer eligible once they attain $2,000 in countable resources. However, two current initiatives allow eligible recipients to accumulate assets above that limit. These are the SSI initiative Plans for Achieving Self Support (PASS) and, separately, Individual Development Accounts (IDAs). Either one of these might be modified to include provisions that target recipients in foster care.

Plans for Achieving Self-Support (PASS)

A Plan for Achieving Self-Support (PASS) is an individual plan for employment designed by an SSI beneficiary with the assistance of a state vocational rehabilitation agency, disability service organization or Ticket to Work Employment Network and approved by the SSA. A PASS must include a specific goal for employment, such as a specific job type desired or a plan for setting up a small business and must include a time line for achieving the employment goal. The PASS must also include a list and cost of any goods, such as assistive devices or job-specific tools, or services, such as schooling, that will be needed by the beneficiary to achieve his or her goal.

Resources included in an approved PASS are not counted against the SSI resource limits. There is no limit to the amount of resources that can be excluded as part of a PASS and these resources can include money set aside to pay for elements of the PASS such as training or items purchased as part of the PASS such as assistive technology devices.

Individual Development Accounts (IDAs)

Individual Development Accounts (IDAs) are matched savings accounts that allow families and persons with low incomes to set aside money for education, the purchase of a home, or the creation of a business.[96] An individual may place money from his or her earnings into an IDA and have that amount of money matched by the state with funds from the state's Temporary Assistance for Needy Families (TANF) block grant or by certain state and local government agencies or non-profit organizations.[97]

Money saved in a qualified IDA, including the state contribution and any interest earned, is not counted as a resource for the purposes of determining SSI eligibility.[98] There is no limit to the amount of money in an IDA that can be excluded from the SSI resource calculation. However, there are limits to the amounts states and other entities can contribute to IDAs.[99]

End Notes

[1] Erik Eckholm, "Welfare Agency Seeks Children's Assets," *New York Times*, February 17, 2006, p. A-1.

[2] *In the Matter of J.M.G., appeal docketed*, No. COA06-752 (N.C. Ct. App. June 7, 2006) available at http://www.aoc.state

[3] Estimate based on the Congressional Research Service's (CRS) analysis of data reported for FY2007 to the U.S. Department of Health and Human Services (HHS) via the Adoption and Foster Care Analysis Reporting System (AFCARS, FY2007). Forty-eight states and the District of Columbia were able to report data on receipt of SSI or other Social Security Act benefits (e.g., Title II benefits) for children in foster care on the last day of FY2007. Among those 49 jurisdictions, 29,004 children (6.1% of all children in their care) were reported as receiving an SSI/other SSA benefit. This includes 2,281 children in Florida (8.7% of state's caseload), which indicated that its report was based on *eligibility for SSI/other SSA benefits rather than actual receipt of those benefits.* Data on receipt of SSI/other SSA benefits were missing for all foster care children in Alaska and nearly all foster care children in Maryland. Puerto Rico is not eligible to operate an SSI program and its caseload data were excluded from the analysis.

[4] Kerry DeVooght, Tiffany Allen, and Rob Geen, *Federal, State, and Local Spending to Address Child Abuse and Neglect in SFY 2006*, Child Trends, December 2008, p. 19, at http://www.childtrends.org/Files//Child_Trends2009_02_17_FR_CWFinancePaper.pdf. State-level data were provided by Child Trends to the Congressional Research Service, January 2009. (Hereafter DeVooght, Allen, and Geen, *Federal, State, and Local Spending to Address Child Abuse and Neglect in SFY 2006*, Child Trends, December 2008.)

[5] *Washington State Department of Social and Health Services v. Guardianship Estate of Danny Keffeler*, hereafter *Keffeler*, 537 U.S. 371 (2003).

[6] Throughout this report, references to titles, parts, or sections of the law refer to the Social Security Act, unless otherwise explicitly stated.

[7] With an exception, discussed below, the income and asset tests, as well as family structure/living arrangement rules are identical to the federal /state rules that applied to the now-defunct cash aid program, Aid to Families with Dependent Children (AFDC), as they existed on July 16, 1996. Under the prior law AFDC program, states established specific AFDC income and asset rules (within some federal parameters). The federal AFDC asset limit was $1,000, however, P.L. 106-169 raised the allowable counted asset limit to $10,000 for purposes of determining Title IV-E eligibility. In addition to meeting the income/asset criteria in the home from which he/she was removed, a child must meet the AFDC family structure/living arrangement rules. Those rules granted eligibility primarily to children in single-parent families (parents are divorced, separated, or never-married and one spouse is not living with the child; or the parent is dead). In some cases a child in a two-parent family may be eligible (if one parent meets certain unemployment criteria).

[8] Section 475(4)(A) of the act (42 U.S.C. § 675(4)(A) as amended by P.L. 110-351. Section 8.3B. 1 of the *Child Welfare Policy Manual* of the Children's Bureau, Administration for Children, Youth and Families (ACYF), Administration for Children and Families (ACF), Department of Health and Human Services (hereafter referred to as the *Child Welfare Policy Manual)* further discusses allowable federal foster care maintenance payment costs and is available at http://www.acf.hhs.gov/j2ee/programs/cb/laws

[9] Each state's FMAP is determined annually by a specified formula. For FY20 10, the maximum FMAP for Title IV-E foster care purposes is just under 76% (Mississippi). For more information, see http://aspe.hhs.gov/health. Each state's FMAP is determined annually by a formula specified in statute. In general, a state's FMAP may be no lower than 50% (in states with the highest per capita income) and no higher than 83% (in states with lower per capita income). During FY20 10, however, the American Recovery and Reinvestment Act (P.L. 111-5) increased the annually calculated FMAP rate for Title IV-E purposes by a little more than 6% in all states (i.e., no state receives FMAP of less than about 56%). For more information on statutory FMAP formula, see http://aspe.hhs.gov/health/fmap.htm, and for more information on the increased rate provided by ARRA, see CRS Report R4021 1, *Human Services Provisions of the American Recovery and Reinvestment Act*, by Gene Falk et al.

[10] Expenditure and average maintenance payment estimates are based on Congressional Research Service analysis of state Title IV-E foster care expenditure claims made in FY2008, as compiled by the U.S. Department of Health and Human Services (HHS), Administration for Children and Families (ACF), May 2009. Maintenance payment cost reimbursed by child support payments are excluded; data from Puerto Rico are excluded because Puerto Rico is unable to document Title IV-E eligibility and it did not submit current claims. Florida and California were excluded (from calculation of average payments only) because, under Title IV-E waivers, these states receive all, or a sizeable portion, of their Title IV-E foster care maintenance payment funding as part of a pre-negotiated lump sum that may be spent on multiple purposes (and without regard to Title IV-E eligibility).

[11] U.S. Department of Health and Human Services (HHS), Administration for Children and Families (ACF), state foster care expenditure claim data for FY2008, May 2009.

[12] Section 471(a)(17). Among other reasons, a state may determine that seeking child support payments is not "appropriate" for a foster child, if it might impede efforts to reunite the child with the parent . See *Child Welfare Policy Manual*, Section 8.4C, Question 2.

[13] Section 457(e). See, also, 45 CFR 302.52.

[14] Section 457(e) (2) provides that state "may" use the funds in this manner. However federal regulations (45 CFR 302.52(b)(2)) provide that the funds "must" be used in this manner.

[15] U.S. Department of Health and Human Services (HHS), Administration for Children and Families (ACF), state Title IV-E foster care expenditure claims for FY2007, May 2008.

Most of this child welfare waiver funding was distributed to three states (California: $425 million; Florida: $150 million; and Illinois: $50 million).

[16] Under a 1979 U.S. Supreme Court ruling in *Miller v. Youakim* (444 U.S. 125 (1979)), states are not permitted to make a lesser foster care maintenance payment on behalf of a Title IV-E eligible child placed with a relative than the state would pay for that same child if he/she were placed with a non-relative. This rule, however, does not apply with regard to foster care children who are not eligible for Title IV-E foster care support. Under the Temporary Assistance for Needy Families (TANF) block grant, states may provide a "child-only" benefit for relatives (e.g., a grandparent) caring for a child. As long as the grant is solely for the child (no funds are provided for an adult in the household), the income and resources of the relative's home do not need to be considered. However, TANF child-only benefits are typically less generous than foster care maintenance payments.

[17] There are some situations where federal statute would also permit a state agency to use TANF (Title IV-A) to make foster care payments and many states are believed to use this authority. However, these federal block grant funds are primarily provided for non-foster care purposes and, in order for the child welfare agency to have access to them must be allocated to the agency (by the state legislature).

[18] Other federal sources of funds, which are not dedicated solely to foster care purposes but which might be accessed for some part of the cost of case planning or services to children in foster care include Title XIX (Medicaid), Title XX (Social Services Block Grant) and Title IV-A (TANF). See Cynthia Scarcella Andrews, et. al, *The Cost of Protecting Vulnerable Children V*, (Washington, DC: Urban Institute), May 2006.

[19] U.S. Department of Health and Human Services, Adoption and Foster Care Analysis Reporting System (AFCARS) Report #16 (Preliminary Estimates for FY2008) (October 2009), available at http://www.acf.hhs.gov/programs/cb/stats_research/afcars/tar

[20] States may continue to make claims for a youth who has reached his/her 1 8th birthday only if the youth is still completing high school or a GED and has not reached 19 years of age. See, Section 8.3A.2 of the *Child Welfare Policy Manual* available at http://www.acf.hhs.gov/j2ee/programs/cb/laws

[21] States are reimbursed based on their Federal Medical Assistance Percentage (FMAP), which may range from 50%, in states with the highest per capita income, to a maximum of 83%, in states with the lowest per capita income.

[22] These programs are authorized at Section 477 of the act (42 U.S.C. § 677).

[23] These programs are authorized at Section 477 of the act (42 U.S.C. § 677).

[24] States may continue to provide an Education and Training Voucher to a youth already using the program, so long as the youth is successfully enrolled in a post-secondary education or training program, until the youth's 23rd birthday. Education and Training Vouchers may be valued at up to $5,000/year, and these funds may be used to defray any room or board expense that would be considered a "cost of attendance" under Section 472 of the Higher Education Act (20 U.S.C. § 1087ll). In addition, states may spend no more than 30% of their general Chafee funding for room and board costs of youth who have reached their 18th birthday and have not passed their 21st birthday.

[25] For more information see the Social Security Administration (SSA) publication *Benefits for Children* available on the website of SSA at http://www.ssa.gov/pubs/10085.pdf; and CRS Report RS22294, *Social Security Survivors Benefits*, by Kathleen Romig and Scott Szymendera.

[26] For more information, see the SSA publication *Benefits for Children with Disabilities* available on the website of SSA at http://www.ssa.gov/pubs/10026.pdf; and CRS Report RL32279, *Primer on Disability Benefits: Social Security Disability Insurance (SSDI) and Supplemental Security Income (SSI)*, by Scott Szymendera.

[27] SSI benefits are not available to residents of Puerto Rico, Guam, or the United States Virgin Islands. Residents of these jurisdictions are eligible to receive federal benefits from their commonwealth or territorial government under provisions of Title XIV and Title XVI of the

Social Security Act. These benefits are administered by the U.S. Department of Health and Human Services.

[28] 42 U.S.C. § 1382c(a)(3)(C)(I).

[29] The rules for deeming of income and resources are complex and can vary by state. For more information see the SSA publication *Understanding Supplemental Security Income (SSI)* available on the website of SSA at http://www.socialsecurity.gov/notices/supplemental-security

[30] 42 U.S.C. § 1382(a).

[31] The SSI resource exclusions can be found in Section 1613 of the act (42 USC § 1382b) and in the Code of Federal Regulations at 20 CFR 416.1210-416.1239.

[32] Under Section 472(a) of the Social Security Act, foster children who receive Title IV-E foster care maintenance payments and do not receive SSI may accumulate up to $10,000 in assets. See page 25 for further discussion of this provision.

[33] Back benefits are often the result of delays in the disability determination process.

[34] Other items, approved in advance by the SSA, may be purchased using money from a dedicated account.

[35] These guidelines, as well as procedures used by SSA to ensure compliance are found in Sections 205(j) and 1632(a)(2) of the act (42 U.S.C. §§ 405(j) and 1383(a)(2)).

[36] Social Security Administration, *Annual Statistical Supplement to the Social Security Bulletin, 2008*, Washington, DC, March, 2009, Tables 5.L1 and 7.E4.

[37] 20 C.F.R. §§ 404.2010 and 416.610.

[38] This order of selection differs for adults, adults with drug or alcohol problems, and children. The complete orders of selection can be found at 20 C.F.R. §§ 404.2021 and 416. 621.

[39] POMS GN 00502.159.

[40] 42 U.S.C. §§ 405(j)(1)(A) and 1383(a)(2)(A)(I).

[41] 20 C.F.R. §§ 404.235(a) and 416.635(a).

[42] 20 C.F.R. §§ 404.2040(a) and 416. 640(a).

[43] 42 U.S.C. §§ 405(j)(2)(C)(i)(III) and 1383(a)(2)(B)(iii)(III).

[44] 42 U.S.C. §§ 405(j)(2)(C)(iii)(III) and 1383(a)(2)(B)(v)(III).

[45] 20 C.F.R. §§ 404.2040(d) and 416.640(d).

[46] Social Security Administration, *SSI Annual Statistical Report, 2008*, Washington, DC, September 2009, Table 17. Available online at http://www.ssa.gov/policy. In 2007, there were nearly 74 million (73,941,848) children under age 18 in the U.S. Census data from 2008 are available at http://factfinder.census.gov/servlet/DTTable?_bm=y&-state PEP_2008_EST_G2008_T008_2008&-CONTEXT=dt&-redoLog=true&-geo_id=01000US&-format=&-_lang=en.

[47] Social Security Administration, *SSI Annual Statistical Report, 2008*, Washington, DC, September 2009, Table 19. For 2.3% of the children, their disability was unknown. The primary function of the SSA's disability determination process is to determine an individual's eligibility for benefits, and not make any specific diagnosis. For research purposes, the SSA groups SSI applicants and recipients based on its own diagnostic classifications which are loosely based on the *International Classification of Diseases: 9th revision, Clinical Modification*, 4th ed., more commonly referred to as the ICD-9 codes.

[48] National Survey of Child and Adolescent Well-Being. "Estimates of Supplemental Security Income Eligibility for Children in out of Home Placements." Research Brief No. 12. Available online at http://www.acf.hhs.gov/programs/opre/abuse_neglect/nscaw/reports/est_suppl/est_suppl.pdf . See also U.S. Department of Health and Human Services, Administration for Children and Families, National Survey of Child and Adolescent Well-being (NSCAW), *One Year in Foster Care, Wave 1 Data Analysis Report*, (Washington: GPO 2003), pp. 13, 20. See also Susan dos Reis, et al, "Mental Health Services for Youths in Foster Care and Disabled Youths." *American Journal of Public Health,* July 2001, pp.1094-1099; and Susan Kools

and Christine Kennedy, "Foster Child Health and Development: Implications for Primary Care," *Pediatric Nursing,* January-February 2003, pp. 39-46.

49 Informal survey conducted by APHSA in 2006. Data provided to CRS in personal communications. Most states said that the procedures used to make applications were applicable on a statewide (as opposed to county level) basis and, at least nine states said that the child's expected length of stay in foster care was a factor in the procedures.

50 The *Child Welfare Policy Manual* is issued by the U.S. Department of Health and Human Services, Administration for Children and Families.

51 Section 8.4D - Question 1 of the *Child Welfare Policy Manual.* At the same time, a state may make Title IV-E *administrative* claims on behalf of a child who is Title IV-E eligible but who is also SSI-eligible and receives only an SSI benefit and this federal program support will *not* reduce the SSI benefit. (See Question 3 of the same Section.)

52 POMS SI 00830.410.

53 Section 8.4D - Question 2, *Child Welfare Policy Manual.*

54 APHSA survey.

55 SSDI and Survivor's benefits are based on a disabled or deceased individual's past average monthly earnings. Benefits are provided to dependents (such as spouses or children), subject to certain maximum family benefit limits.

56 DeVooght, Allen, and Geen, *Federal, State, and Local Spending to Address Child Abuse and Neglect in SFY 2006*, Child Trends, December 2008, p. 19.

57 The total foster care caseload data includes the 50 states and the District of Columbia for FY2006 as provided by the U.S. Department of Health and Human Services (HHS) to the Congressional Research Service, February 2009.

58 This estimate was made by the Congressional Research Service by calculating the average annual dollar amount per child in foster care that was spent from Social Security benefits among states reporting data ($514) and applying that dollar amount to the number of children in foster care from non-reporting states (excluding Puerto Rico).

59 *Keffeler*, 537 U.S. 371 (2003).

60 145 Wn.2d.1 (2001).

61 878 F.2d. 263 (9th Cir. 1989).

62 *Keffeler*, 537 U.S. 371 (2003), pp. 8-10.

63 Ibid., p. 9, which cites Section 207(a) of the act (42 U.S.C. § 407(a)). This section of the act is commonly referred to as the anti-attachment clause because it protects Social Security benefits from "execution, levy, attachment, garnishment, or other legal process."

64 *Keffeler*, 537 U.S. 371 (2003), pp. 12-13.

65 Ibid., pp. 13 -14, referencing, 20 C.F.R. § 404.2040 and 20 C.F.R.§416.640(a).

66 Ibid., p. 16.

67 Ibid., p. 17.

68 As provided in federal regulations, the stated purpose of the SSI program is to "assure a minimum level of income for people who are age 65 or over, or who are blind or disabled and who do not have sufficient income and resources to maintain a standard of living at the established Federal minimum income level "(20 C.F.R. § 416.110). The stated purpose of the Social Security benefit programs is to provide beneficiaries with "income required for ordinary and necessary living expenses" (20 C.F.R § 404.508(a)).

69 *Keffeler*, 537 U.S. 371 (2003), p. 17.

70 For a summary of the arguments made by the opposing sides in this case see Elizabeth Oppenheim, "Funding for Children in Foster Care: The *Keffeler* Case," *Policy & Practice of Public Human Services*, March 2003, pp. 22-28.

71 Patrick Gardner. "*Keffeler* v DSHS: Picking the Pockets of America's Neediest Children," *Youth Law News*, July- September, 2002, p. 12. (Hereafter "Picking the Pockets.") In its *Keffeler* opinion, the U.S. Supreme Court noted that *Keffeler* charged the state with "failing to exercise discretion in how it uses benefits, periodically 'sweeping' beneficiaries' accounts to pay for past care and 'double dipping' by using benefits to reimburse the state

for costs previously recouped from other sources." These charges, the Court noted were "far afield" of the issue on which it had agreed to hear the case. It noted, however, that these alleged improper uses of payments were concerns that could be brought to the Commissioner on Social Security "who bears responsibility for overseeing representative payees or elsewhere as appropriate." Subsequently, the Washington State Supreme Court, in *Guardianship Estate of Danny Keffeler v. The Department of Social and Health Services* (151 Wn. 2d. 331 (2004), a case that looked at certain constitutional claims made by *Keffeler*, concurred with the U.S. Supreme Court.

[72] Daniel L. Hatcher, "Foster Care Children Paying for Foster Care," *Cardozo Law Review*, vol. 27, no. 4 (2006), p. 1835. (Hereafter "Foster Care Children Paying for Foster Care"). Lawyers on behalf of *Keffeler* argued that differences between foster children with private representative payees and those with agency representative payees amounted to a violation of the Constitution's equal protection clause. Those claims were addressed in the 2004 decision, by the Washington Supreme Court (145 Wn. 331). The court disagreed noting that the duties of the representative payees were the same in any case.

[73] Jim Moye, "Get Your Hands Out of Their Pockets: The Case Against State Seizure of Foster Children's Social Security Benefits," *Georgetown Journal on Poverty Law & Policy*, Winter 2003, p. 5. See also "Foster Care Children Paying for Foster Care," p. 1814.

[74] Ibid., p. 1814.

[75] "Picking the Pockets," p. 10.

[76] Brief by Children's Defense Fund, et. al, as Amici Curiae Supporting Petitioners (August 2, 2002) p. 14 in *Washington State Department of Social and Health Services v. Guardianship Estate of Danny Keffeler,* (No. 01-1420). (Hereafter referenced as "Brief by Children's Defense Fund et al.")

[77] Brief by the State of Florida et al. as Amici Curiae Supporting Petitioners (August 2, 2002), p. 7 in *Washington State Department of Social and Health Services v. Guardianship Estate of Danny Keffeler* 537 U.S. 371 (2003) (No. 01- 1420).

[78] *Keffeler*, 537 U.S. 371 (2003), p. 18.

[79] Brief by Children's Defense Fund, et al., pp. 20-24.

[80] Ibid., p. 22.

[81] *Keffeler*, 537 U.S. 371 (2003), p. 19.

[82] Brief by the counties of California—Los Angeles, San Bernardino, Santa Clara, Contra Costa, Alameda, Modoc, Napa, Nevada, Riverside, San Diego, Tulare—and the California State Association of Counties, as Amici Curiae Supporting Petitioners, pp. 16-18 in *Washington State Department of Social and Health Services v. Guardianship Estate of Danny Keffeler* 537 U.S. 371 (2003) (No. 01-1420).

[83] The Social Security Protection Act (P.L. 108-203) provided additional safeguards for Social Security and SSI beneficiaries with representative payees and enhanced program protections. However, the legislation did not address selection of representative payees for foster children.

[84] 2005 Cal. Stat. 641. A copy of the legislation (AB 1633) can be found on the website of the California Assembly at http://www.leginfo.ca.gov/pub/05-06/bill/asm/ab_1601-1650/ab_1633_bill_20051007_chaptered.pdf.

[85] The practice of passing through child support payments to families was originally enacted under the Aid to Families with Dependent Children (AFDC) program in 1975 (P.L. 93-647). The purpose of this practice was to fill the gap between the needs standard established by a state (or the amount the state determined that a family of a certain size would need to subsist) and the actual amount needed to subsist, if necessary.

[86] For more information see CRS Report RS22380, *Child Support Enforcement: Program Basics*, by Carmen Solomon- Fears.

[87] CRS Report RL34 105, *The Financial Impact of Child Support on TANF Families: Simulation for Selected States*, by Carmen Solomon-Fears and Gene Falk; and Center for Law and

Social Policy, "State Child Support Pass-Through Policies, by Michelle Vinson and Vicki Turetsky, June 12, 2009.

88 *Hearing to Review Proposals to Improve Child Protective Services before the House Committee on Ways and Means, Subcommittee on Human Resources*, 109th Cong., 2nd sess., 2006 (statement of Daniel L. Hatcher).

89 "Foster Care Children Paying for Foster Care," p. 1845.

90 See 20 C.F.R. §§ 404.2021 and 416.521.

91 "Foster Care Children Paying for Foster Care," p. 1845.

92 For additional information about the CASA Program, see CRS Report RL32976, *Child Welfare: Programs Authorized by the Victims of Child Abuse Act of 1990*, by Emilie Stoltzfus.

93 42 U.S.C. § 1382(a).

94 "Foster Care Children Paying for Foster Care," p. 1846.

95 U.S. Congress, House Committee on Ways and Means, *Foster Care Independence Act of 1999*, report to accompany H.R. 1802, 106th Cong., 1st Sess., H.Rept. 106-182, (Washington: GPO 1999), p. 29.

96 For additional information on IDAs, see CRS Report RS221 85, *Individual Development Accounts (IDAs): Background and Current Legislation for Federal Grant Programs to Help Low-Income Families Save*, by Gene Falk.

97 Under the provisions of the Assets for Independence Act, P.L. 105-285, non-profit organizations and state, local, or tribal governments may compete for grants to fund IDAs for low-income households. IDAs funded through this program are often called Demonstration Project IDAs while IDAs funded through the TANF program are often referred to as TANF IDAs.

98 There are other types of IDAs that are targeted to specific groups, including refugees and persons living in assisted housing. However, only TANF and Demonstration Project IDAs are exempt from the SSI resource rules.

99 For additional information on these limits, see CRS Report RS22 185, *Individual Development Accounts (IDAs): Background and Current Legislation for Federal Grant Programs to Help Low-Income Families Save*, by Gene Falk.

In: Child Welfare: Federal Role in Assistance... ISBN: 978-1-61209-704-6
Editors: M.G. Raposo, D.M. Carroca © 2011 Nova Science Publishers, Inc.

Chapter 3

CHILD WELFARE: RECENT AND PROPOSED FEDERAL FUNDING

Emilie Stoltzfus

SUMMARY

Child welfare services and supports are intended to ensure and improve the safety, permanence, and well-being of children. The President's FY2011 budget seeks close to $8.5 12 billion for the child welfare programs discussed in this report. This request is $80 million above the FY2010 funding appropriated for those programs as part of the Consolidated Appropriations Act, 2010 (P.L. 111-117). Congress has not yet finalized FY2011 appropriations. However, on September 30, 2010, President Obama signed the Continuing Appropriations Act, 2011 (P.L. 111-242). That law generally extends federal funding, at the levels provided in FY20 10, until December 3, 2010, or until full-year funding is enacted, whichever happens first. For child welfare programs, the Senate Appropriations Committee has recommended full-year FY20 11 funding at a level similar to the President's request. Most child welfare programs are administered by the Administration for Children and Families (ACF) within the Department of Health and Human Services (HHS). However, a few are administered by the Office of Justice Programs at the Department of Justice.

As requested in the President's FY2011 budget, Congress acted to extend (for six months) enhanced federal support to states for costs they incur in providing foster care maintenance, adoption assistance, and kinship guardianship assistance payments under Title IV-E of the Social Security Act (H.R. 1586, P.L. 111-226). Unlike the President's request, the bill approved by Congress will step down the level of enhanced support during those six months. HHS estimates the enacted legislation will result in an additional $75 million in federal support to states under Title IV-E. The President's FY20 11 budget also sought legislation to continue for one year the FY20 10 level of mandatory funding for two grants that support efforts to improve state court handling of child welfare proceedings ($20 million), as well as annual mandatory funding to continue the National Survey of Child and Adolescent Well-Being ($6 million). Congress included both of those proposals, with full-year (FY20 11) funding, in the recently enacted P.L. 111-242.

The President's FY2011 budget proposes to redirect all the discretionary funds provided under the Adoption Awareness program ($13 million for FY20 10) to the Adoption Opportunities program. The Senate Appropriations Committee reported legislation (S. 3686, S.Rept. 111-243) that would follow this recommendation. Further, the President's FY2011 budget seeks $10 million in new discretionary appropriations to advance state implementation of evidence-based programs or activities to prevent child abuse and neglect, and an additional $2.5 million (for a total of $42 million) in FY2011 funds to fully support Adoption Incentives for states that increase adoptions from foster care. The Senate Appropriations Committee recommends funding to meet both of those requests (S.Rept. 111-243). Finally, while the President's FY2011 budget proposes $10 million in funding for Court Appointed Special Advocates (down from $15 million for FY2010) and $20 million for Children's Advocacy Centers (down from $22.5 million for FY2010), the Senate Appropriations Committee recommends maintaining Children's Advocacy Center funding at $22.5 million for FY2011 and would provide $14.2 in federal CASA funds (S.Rept. 111-229).

About 86% ($7.2 billion) of the $8.4 billion in federal funds provided in FY20 10 for child welfare purposes supports states' provision of foster care and adoption or kinship guardianship assistance; 9% ($778 million) is distributed to all states for child and family services; more than 2% ($185 million) is for services to assist youth who have left or are expected to leave foster care because of their age; and about 3% ($228 million) is for child welfare related competitive grants or awards. **Table 1** shows the share of dedicated child welfare funding provided by general category for recent years and as proposed for FY2011. **Table 2** includes recent and proposed funding levels by child welfare program.

Child welfare services are intended to prevent the abuse or neglect of children, to ensure that children have safe, permanent homes; and to promote the well-being of children and their families. Most federal child welfare programs are administered by the Administration for Children and Families (ACF) within the U.S. Department of Health and Human Services (HHS). Funding for ACF programs is primarily provided in the annual appropriations bill for the Departments of Labor, HHS, and Education. Several child welfare programs (authorized by the Victims of Child Abuse Act) are administered by the Office of Justice Programs (OJP) within the Department of Justice. Their funding is provided in the annual appropriations bill for the Departments of Commerce and Justice.

FY2011 Budget Request and Congressional Action

The FY2011 budget request submitted by the Obama Administration in February 2010 seeks $8.512 billion in federal funding for child welfare related programs. This amount includes $7.313 billion for foster care, adoption assistance, and kinship guardianship assistance under Title IV-E of the Social Security Act and an additional $185 million in funding for support of youth who have made or are expected to make the transition from state foster care custody to adulthood without benefit of placement in a permanent family. The President's proposed budget would also provide $788 million for formula grants to states dedicated to provision of services to children and families that strengthen families, prevent unnecessary removal of children from their homes, and enable children in foster care to be reunited with their parents or to find another permanent home. Finally, the budget would provide $236 million primarily for competitive grants to support research, demonstration, technical assistance and other activities designed to improve child welfare services.

FY2011 began on October 1, 2010 and, as of the October recess, Congress had not yet approved full FY2011 appropriations levels. However, in late September it passed the Continuing Appropriations Act, 2011 (H.R. 3081), to temporarily permit the release of federal funding in the new fiscal year. President Obama signed the short-term funding measure into law on September 30, 2010 (P.L. 111-242). Generally, the law continues funding at the FY20 10 funding levels for given child welfare programs and will remain in effect until December 3, 2010, or until a full FY2011 funding bill is enacted—whichever comes first. As of October 2010, the House

Appropriations Committee had not yet formally reported FY2011 appropriations legislation for HHS or the Justice Department. The Senate Appropriations Committee reported legislation to fund Justice Department programs on July 22, 2010 (S. 3636, S.Rept. 111-229), and to fund HHS programs on August 2, 2010 (S. 3686, S.Rept. 111-243). That committee-reported legislation would provide a certain sum of $8.254 billion for the child welfare programs discussed in this report.

On August 10, 2010, the President signed H.R. 1586, popularly known as the Education jobs and Medicaid funding bill, into law (P.L. 111-226); it authorizes continued enhanced funding for certain payments made under the Title IV-E foster care, adoption assistance, and kinship guardianship assistance program for an additional six months (January 2011 through June 2011) but would step down that level of increased support across that time frame.

Legislative Proposals

Legislative proposals are included in the President's budget when, apart from appropriating the necessary funds, legislative authority does not exist for the Administration to carry out the proposal in FY2011.

Proposal for Six-Month Extension of Enhanced Title IV-E Support to States

Under the American Recovery and Reinvestment Act (P.L. 111-5), the federal government is temporarily (October 1, 2008 through December 31, 2010) required to pay a larger share of the costs incurred by a state to provide foster care maintenance, adoption assistance, and kinship guardianship assistance payments for eligible children. The level of enhanced support included in ARRA (for purposes of Title IV-E) was equal to 6.1 percentage points.[1] The President's FY2011 budget sought to extend that same level of enhanced federal support through June 30, 2011. In August, Congress acted to extend enhanced federal support for the six months requested, but it provided a lower, or phased-down, level of enhanced support. Specifically, the popularly titled Education jobs and Medicaid bill (H.R. 1586, enacted as P.L. 111-226 on August 10, 2010) provides enhanced federal support equal to 3.2 percentage points for the first three months of calendar year 2011 and 1.2 percentage points for the second three months.[2] After June 30, 2010, the level of federal participation in the Title IV-E program is scheduled to return to normal. HHS estimates that P.L. 111-226 will increase federal support provided to states under Title IV-E by $75 million. By contrast, HHS had earlier estimated that extending the full ARRA level of enhanced federal support across those six months would have resulted in an additional $237 million in federal Title IV-E support. (That latter amount is included in the $7.313 billion request for Title IV-E noted above.) [3]

Request for Authority to Continue Mandatory Funding for Certain Programs

Additional proposals included in the FY2011 budget request call for legislative authority to continue, for one year, mandatory funding for (1) grants to states' highest courts to improve training and data collection and analysis related to child welfare proceedings ($20 million);[4] and (2) research related to characteristics and experiences of children at risk of, or who have experienced, child abuse and neglect ($6 million).[5] As part of the recently enacted temporary funding extension (P.L. 111-242), Congress enacted both of these proposals.

Proposals to Increase, Reduce, or Redirect Child Welfare Funds

Certain proposals to increase, reduce, or redirect funding do not require Congressional program authorization to be carried out. However, they generally require Congress to appropriate funds in different amounts or in different ways than in previous years. The Senate Appropriations Committee has recommended that the President's request for increased funding for child abuse and neglect prevention research be provided and that, also as requested by the President, funding for two adoption related programs be moved to a single account (S.Rept. 111-243). However, it recommends a smaller reduction in funding to the Court Appointed Special Advocates (CASA) program than requested by the President and it would not reduce the Children's Advocacy Center below the FY20 10 funding level as requested by the President (S.Rept. 111-229). The President's proposals and the Senate Appropriations Committee recommendations are discussed further below.

Proposed Grants Related to Prevention of Child Abuse and Neglect

The President's FY2011 budget seeks an additional discretionary appropriation of $10 million to "establish a new competitive grant program for states to support increased use and high quality implementation of evidence-based and evidence-informed child maltreatment prevention programs and activities," including use of existing funding streams to support community-based prevention activities. The competitive grant program is expected to support 8 to 10 grants and would also be used to "insure that child maltreatment prevention and family support is integrated with other state systems for children and youth."[6] These funds are requested under the authority of the Child Abuse Prevention and Treatment Act (CAP TA). That act requires HHS to support research related to the identification, assessment, prevention, and treatment of child abuse and neglect. Therefore, apart from Congress agreeing to appropriate these funds, no additional Congressional authority is necessary to implement this Administration proposal.

The Senate Appropriations Committee recommends providing $10 million, as requested, for this purpose and adds that the program will "focus on families with very young children who are at the greatest risk of child maltreatment, and will include evidence-based prevention strategies to promote parental resilience, knowledge of parenting and child development, nurturing and attachment, concrete support, and social connections." Although it recommends the full $10 million for the proposed grants in FY2011, the Senate Appropriations Committee recommended overall spending for the CAPTA appropriations account that supports research and demonstration projects (child abuse discretionary activities) at about $1.7 million less than what the President requested (i.e., it recommends $37.3 million in funds as opposed to $39.0 million requested in the Administration's FY2011 budget). In addition, the Senate Appropriations Committee would direct HHS/ACF to spend an additional $1.45 million from this same account for seven specific projects in as many states.[7]

Request to Redirect Adoption Awareness Funding to Adoption Opportunities

The President's FY20 11 budget proposes to end the Adoption Awareness program and to redirect funding that has been provided for that program ($13 million in FY20 10) to the Adoption Opportunities program. The Adoption Opportunities program was established in 1978 (P.L. 95- 266) to support research, demonstration projects, and other activities that reduce barriers to the adoption of children, particularly children with special needs. Funding authority for this program expired with FY2008 but Congress has continued to provide support. For FY2010, the program received $26 million.[8] The Adoption Awareness program, established by the Children's Health Act of

2000 (P.L. 106-310), authorizes HHS to make competitive grants for infant adoption awareness,[9] and special needs adoption awareness.[10] Funding authority for both components of the Adoption Awareness program expired with FY2005 but Congress has continued to provide support.[11] For FY2010, the program received $13 million.

The President's FY2011 budget would redirect the $13 million provided for Adoption Awareness programs in FY2010 to the Adoption Opportunities program for FY2011. Combined with its prior funding level, this would bring Adoption Opportunities funding for FY2011 to $39 million. In justifying this request, the Administration states that the Adoption Opportunities program includes "broad authority to fund projects supporting adoption, including projects similar to those under the Children's Health Act programs such as assuring adoption awareness among pregnant women. Consolidating these funds will provide a more efficient mechanism for financing projects and will allow the Administration to target adoption funds to a broader range of grantees and adoption purposes."[12]

The Senate Appropriations Committee "agrees with this consolidation." It recommends $39 million for Adoption Opportunities and would provide no funding for Adoption Awareness, which it describes as "eliminated" in the budget request. [13]

Increased Funding Requested for Adoption Incentives

The President's FY2011 budget seeks $42 million in discretionary appropriations for the Adoption Incentive program, which is $2.5 million more than funding provided ($39.5 million) in the FY20 10 appropriations act (P.L. 111-117). The Senate Appropriations Committee recommends providing this full amount to "fully fund adoption incentives earned by States under current law."[14] For FY2009, states increased the number of children adopted out of foster care to about 55,700 and funds available to make Adoption Incentive awards in September 2010 were not sufficient to pay the full bonuses earned. (See "Adoption Incentives," below, for more information on recent awards made.)

Reduced Funding Proposed for Two Programs

The President's FY2011 budget requests $10 million to support Court Appointed Special Advocates (CASA) as opposed to the $15 million provided for that program for FY20 10. It further proposes $20 million in FY2011 funding for Children's Advocacy Centers, which is $2.5 million less than the $22.5 million provided for FY20 10 (P.L. 111-117). By contrast, the Senate

Appropriations Committee recommends providing $14.2 million for the CASA program in FY2011, slightly less than the program's FY20 10 funding level but more than the Administration's request, and would maintain the FY2010 level of funding for Children Advocacy Centers ($22.5 million). [15] Both programs are authorized under the Victims of Child Abuse Act (established by Title II of P.L. 101-647, 1990) and are administered by the Office of Justice Programs within the U.S. Department of Justice.

Funding for Court Appointed Special Advocates (CASA) is provided to support CASA programs which train volunteers to—at the court's appointment—represent the best interests of children in certain cases, including child welfare related cases. Funds are provided to develop and sustain local CASA programs and for training and technical assistance related to these programs. Funding for the CASA program is authorized at $12 million annually through FY2011. However, Congress appropriated $15 million in each of FY2009 and FY2010 for the support of CASA. The Office of Justice Programs does not provide an explanation for the proposed funding change as part of its request for program funding for FY20 11.[16]

Funding for Children's Advocacy Centers (including related training and technical assistance) is authorized to support local, regional, and national efforts to improve the investigation and prosecution of child abuse and neglect cases, especially to ensure that victims of child abuse or neglect aren't re-traumatized by the handling of these cases. Authorization to fund program activities was set at $20 million for each of FY2004 and FY2005 (P.L. 108-21) and expired with FY2005.[17] However, the program received appropriations of roughly $15 million in each of FY2006 and FY2007, rising to nearly $17 million in FY2008, $20 million in FY2009, and, most recently, $22.5 million in FY2010. The Office of Justice Programs does not provide an explanation for the proposed funding change as part of its request for program funding for FY2011.[18]

Share of Child Welfare Funding by General Purpose

By far the largest share of dedicated federal child welfare funding (roughly 86% in each of the past several fiscal years) is provided to support, or otherwise administer aid to, children who were removed from their birth families primarily due to abuse or neglect. These include eligible children in foster care and eligible children who left foster care for permanent families via adoption or, as authorized by P.L. 110-351, for kinship guardianship. The largest share of this program funding continues to support children in temporary foster care, including related program administration and training costs. However, as shown in **Table 1**, the part of this funding that is appropriated or requested for support of children *leaving* foster care for permanent adoptive or guardianship homes has been growing while the share appropriated or requested under the Title IV-E program for children in foster care has been in corresponding decline.

In recent years, roughly 9% of federal funding dedicated to child welfare purposes has been appropriated for distribution to all states via formula grants for child welfare-related services to children and families. This remains true for the FY20 11 budget request. These funds are authorized under the Child Abuse Prevention and Treatment Act (CAPTA, Title 1, State Grants and Title II, Community-Based Grants) and under Title IV-B of the Social Security Act (Subpart 1-Stephanie Tubbs Jones Child Welfare Services and Subpart 2-Promoting Safe and Stable Families, PSSF).[19] Funds provided for these programs are used to support services or activities designed to prevent child abuse and neglect; screen and investigate child abuse and neglect allegations; provide family support, family preservation, reunification, and adoption promotion and support services; and improve monthly caseworker visits to children in foster care.

Separately, all states receive formula grant funding under the Chafee Foster Care Independence Program (and related Education and Training Vouchers) to provide services and other support to youth who “age out” of foster care without being placed in a permanent family. Despite an overall decline in the number of children who remain in foster care on the last day of a given fiscal year, the number of children who leave foster care without placement in a permanent home (referred to as “ageing out” or “emancipating” from care) grew from roughly 20,000 during FY2000 to nearly 30,000 during FY2008 (the most recent year for which national data have been published). During that time the annual funding amount dedicated to provide services to these youth ($140 million) has remained unchanged. It represents a little more than 2% of overall funding appropriated or requested for child welfare purposes in recent years. More federal support for older youth who remain in foster care after their 18th birthday (and up to age 21) will be available in states that choose to extend Title IV-E support to these youth.[20] That state option was authorized by P.L. 110-351 and is effective as of the first day of FY2011. States that amend their Title IV-E plans to take this option will be permitted to claim federal support for a part of the costs of providing Title IV-E foster care assistance to eligible youth who choose to remain in foster care past their 18th birthday (up to age 21). Federal Title IV-E funds may then be used to help pay room and board costs for eligible older foster youth and to provide certain program administration and caseworker support to them. However, Title IV-E funds are not generally available to provide services.

Finally, a little less than 3% of federal child welfare funding is requested for competitive grants to public agencies, national or community-based service agencies, research groups, or other eligible entities that provide child and family services or conduct relevant research, including for awards to states that increase the number of children adopted out of foster care. This is consistent with the share of federal funding dedicated to this general child welfare purpose in recent years.

Table 1 shows the final funding, and share of total funding, for each of these general categories as appropriated for FY2009 and FY20 10 and as proposed by the President for FY20 11.

FY2010 APPROPRIATIONS

On December 10, 2009, the House voted 221 to 202 to agree to the conference report accompanying the Consolidated Appropriations Act, 2010 (H.R. 3288, H.Rept. 111-366). The Senate agreed to that same conference report on December 13, 2009, by a vote of 57-35. The legislation was signed into law by the President on December 16, 2009, and became P.L. 111-117.

The law appropriated FY20 10 funds for a broad range of federal agencies, including funding for child welfare programs administered by both HHS and the Department of Justice.

The conference report on the FY20 10 spending measure (H.Rept. 111-366) reconciled differences included in several appropriations acts previously acted on in the House and the Senate. Specifically, Division D of the enacted bill (H.R. 3288, which became P.L. 111-117) funds HHSadministered child welfare programs and reconciled differences between the FY20 10 LaborHHS-Education Appropriations Act (H.R. 3293) as it passed the House in July 2009 and the version of that bill that was reported by the Senate Appropriations Committee in August 2009 (S.Rept. 111-66). In addition, Division B of the FY20 10 omnibus spending measure (P.L. 111- 117) includes funding for

Table 1. Funding Appropriated or Proposed, by General Category ($ in millions; % shown is of total funding provided or proposed)

General Category of Child Welfare Funding	Final FY2009 Funding		Final FY20 10 Funding		President's FY20 11 Request	
FOSTER CARE—Funds to all states to provide foster care for eligible children.[a]	$4,733	57%	$4,681	56%	$4,645	55%
PERMANENCY—Funds to all states to provide adoption assistance or kinship guardianship assistance for eligible children.[a]	$2,342	28%	$2,557	30%	$2,668	31%
CHILD AND FAMILY SERVICES—Funds to all states to improve child protective services and to provide a range of services to children and families.	$768	9%	$778	9%	$778	9%
SERVICES FOR YOUTH—Funds to all states to provide services to youth who are expected to "age out" of foster care and those who have aged out of foster care.	$185	2%	$185	2%	$185	2%
RESEARCH, EVALUATION, TRAINING, DEMONSTRATION and INCENTIVES—Funds for competitive grants to eligible entities to provide child and family services or do research and evaluation related to such services, including prevention of abuse and neglect; and for provision of Adoption Incentives.	$228	3%	$231	3%	$236	3%
Total	$8,257	100%	$8,432	100%	$8,512	100%

Source: Prepared by the Congressional Research Service (CRS). Percentages may not total to 100 because of rounding.

Note: Final sums shown may not equal amounts given in previous versions of this report in instances where HHS used indefinite budget authority to access funds beyond the certain sum authority given in an appropriations bill.

a. The FY2009 and FY20 10 appropriated amounts and the FY20 11 request include funds to meet the enhanced federal share of certain Title IV-E costs as authorized by P.L. 111-5. The FY20 11 funding request also includes funds estimated as necessary to extend that enhanced funding for six months.

several child welfare programs administered by the Justice Department. That division reconciles differences between the version of the FY2010 Commerce-JusticeScience Appropriations Act (H.R. 2847) that passed the House in June 2009 and the version passed by the Senate in November 2009.

Differences in House- or Senate-proposed funding for child welfare programs were relatively limited and in most cases the funding levels provided matched the amounts requested for those programs by President Obama in the FY20 10 budget request. Thus, the enacted legislation generally reflects earlier passed (or Committee-approved) program funding levels. With regard to child welfare related funding, the primary difference between the earlier proposed spending levels in Congress and the Consolidated Appropriations Act, 2010 (P.L. 111-117), relates to support for the current ACF home visiting initiative. Funding for this initiative was not included in the final enacted FY20 10 appropriations legislation. However, as noted below, HHS has announced that the initiative will be continued using funds appropriated to support home visiting (for FY20 10– FY2014) as part of the health care reform legislation that was enacted in March 2010 (P.L. 111- 148).

Funding for the ACF Home Visitation Initiative

The Child Abuse Prevention and Treatment Act (CAPTA) Discretionary Activities account is authorized generally to provide funding for research, technical assistance, demonstration projects, and other activities related to improving the assessment, prevention, and treatment of child abuse and neglect. FY20 10 funding enacted for this account in P.L. 111-117 is less than earlier proposed funding levels because the conference agreement (H.Rept. 111-366) eliminated funding in this account for the existing ACF home visiting initiative, the "Supporting Evidence-Based Home Visiting to Prevent Child Maltreatment." [21] For FY2008 and FY2009, that initiative received funding (of $10 million and $13.5 million, respectively) as a set-aside from the CAPTA discretionary activities account. This set-aside was specified as part of the appropriations process. However, P.L. 111-117 provided no specific funding for the ACF home visiting initiative. Instead, the conferees to the FY20 10 spending measure (H.Rept. 111-366) note that they "anticipate that mandatory funding will be provided for this activity in fiscal year 2010 as proposed by the Administration."[22] Subsequently, as part of health care reform legislation (P.L. 111-148), Congress appropriated funding of $1.5 billion across five years (FY20 1 0–FY20 14), including $100 million for FY20 10, to provide grants to states, territories, and tribes for the support of evidence-based home visiting programs that serve families with young children and those expecting children.[23] HHS has since announced that a portion of the funds appropriated for grants to states to support early childhood home visiting programs will be used to continue this initiative for the full five years it was originally intended to be in place.[24]

FY2011 Budget Request Compared to Past Funding

The President's FY2011 budget request for child welfare programs closely follows funding provided by Congress for those programs in FY20 10 (P.L. 111-117). The largest differences reflect changes in the Administration's estimate of funds needed to reimburse eligible state claims related to foster care, adoption assistance, and guardianship assistance, which is authorized under Title IV-E of the Social Security Act.

The Title IV-E Program

The Obama Administration requests $7.3 13 billion in budget authority for foster care, adoption assistance, and kinship guardianship.[25] This amount includes $237 million in FY20 11 budget authority requested as part of the Administration's legislative proposal to extend (for six months) the enhanced federal support for the Title IV-E program first authorized in the ARRA (P.L. 111-5). However, as noted above, while Congress did extend some additional federal support under Title IV-E for that time period, it did so at a lower rate than what the Administration proposed. HHS estimates that the legislation approved by Congress (H.R. 1586), and enacted on August 10, 2010, (P.L. 111-226) will result in additional federal Title IV-E spending of $75 million. Consequently, in any communications with the Appropriations Committee before enactment of final FY2011 funding, HHS may adjust its request for Title IV-E funding downward (to circa $7. 151 billion) to reflect the changes enacted in P.L. 111-226. However, the discussion below is based on the funding level requested by the Administration in February 2010 (for FY20 11).

The Title IV-E federal foster care, kinship guardianship, and adoption assistance program is authorized on an indefinite basis (i.e., the funding authorization never expires). Title IV-E funding is also authorized on an open-ended entitlement basis. This means the funding provided by Congress for the Title IV-E program must match the federal share of state Title IV-E eligible claims. To ensure adequate funds are annually appropriated for the program, the Administration estimates, each year, how much money will be necessary to reimburse states for the federal share of the eligible foster care, adoption assistance, and kinship guardianship costs they incur. Congress typically provides this definite level of budget authority as part of its annual appropriations process.[26] In the event that the definite amount of funding Congress provides as part of the regular appropriations process exceeds the amount needed to pay the eligible claims submitted by states, these excess funds are eventually returned to the treasury. On the other hand, if the definite sum turns out to be less than the needed amount, HHS may access the additional funds necessary to meet the federal obligations under this program by using the "indefinite" budget authority included in annual appropriations bills. In most years (beginning with FY2002), HHS has needed less funds than were provided in definite budget authority during the annual appropriation process. However, in several recent years, including FY2009 and FY2010, HHS has used this "indefinite" funding authority. This change appears to be primarily related to costs of providing enhanced funding under the ARRA, which were unknown or not fully anticipated at the time of the definite appropriation.

Adoption Assistance

HHS seeks $2.585 billion in Title IV-E adoption assistance funding as part of the FY20 11 appropriations process. This amount is $84 million above the $2.50 1 billion provided by Congress for this Title IV-E program component in FY20 10 (P.L. 111-117)[27] and $247 million more than the federal share of Title IV-E adoption assistance claims submitted by the states in FY2009 ($2.338 billion, the most recent year these data are available). The increased budget authority sought for FY2011 reflects, in part, the increase in federal support made available to states for this program under the ARRA (P.L. 111-5) for the first three months of FY2011 as well as the Administration's legislative proposal to extend this enhanced funding (at 6.1 percentage points) for an additional six months. Further, it is based on the Administration's assumption of a continued increase in the number of children who receive support under the program.

HHS projects the average monthly number of children receiving Title IV-E adoption assistance will grow to 453,900 in FY2011. By comparison, the average monthly number of children receiving federally supported adoption was around 228,300 in FY2000, but had grown to approximately 416,400 children in FY2009.[28] States' continued success in finding permanent adoptive homes for children in foster care combined with changes to federal law that expand federal eligibility for Title IV-E adoption assistance are factors in the caseload growth expected by FY20 11. The number of children adopted with public child welfare agency involvement roughly doubled between FY1995 and FY2000, and since that latter year has been at or above 50,000 each year. In FY2008 (the most recent data available), the number of adoptions of children out of foster care reached an annual recorded high of 55,000. Further, some increase in the Title IV-E adoption assistance caseload is also expected due to continued implementation of the Fostering Connections to Success and Increasing Adoptions Act of 2008 (P.L. 110-351), which broadened eligibility for federal adoption assistance. FY20 11 is the second year of a nine-year phase-in of the new eligibility criteria, which are designed to eventually remove income and resource tests (traditionally tied to a child's *birth* parents) from federal Title IV-E adoption assistance eligibility criteria.[29]

Foster Care

HHS seeks $4.645 billion in Title IV-E foster care funding as part of the FY2011 appropriations process. This is $36 million less than the $4.681 billion in Title IV-E foster care funding included in the FY2010 appropriations bill (P.L. 111-117) but remains $54 million more than the federal share of Title IV-E foster care claims submitted by the states in FY2009 ($4.591 billion, the most recent year these data are available). The primary reason for this decrease in requested funding for FY20 11 is a continued decline in the average monthly number of children receiving Title IV-E foster care assistance. That assumed decline in caseload was strong enough to offset a number of other assumptions that *added* to the estimated cost of Title IV-E foster care assistance in the FY20 11 budget. Finally, those additional assumed costs also help to explain why, despite a larger Title IV-E foster care caseload in FY2009 than is projected for FY2011, states claimed fewer federal Title IV-E foster care dollars for that year than HHS expects them to claim in FY2011.

For FY2011, HHS estimates that an average monthly number of 168,200 children will receive federal foster care assistance. By comparison, some 186,300 children received Title IV-E foster care assistance on an average monthly basis in FY2009 (the most recent year actual data are available) while the comparable number in FY2000 was 287,800.[30] The decline in the number of children receiving Title IV-E foster care assistance is driven by a decrease in the total number of children who are in foster care (those who are eligible for Title IV-E and those who are not) as well as erosion in the share of all children in foster care who meet the Title IV-E eligibility. Those criteria are multifaceted but include an income test. Specifically, a child who is eligible for Title IV-E foster care must have been removed (to foster care) from a home that met the income criteria of a "needy" family under their state's prior law cash welfare program rules as those rules existed in July 1996.[31] Under those rules, the median state need standard (annualized for a family of three) is roughly $7,400, an amount that represents 40% of the federal poverty guideline for a family of that size in 2009. (By comparison, in 1996 this same dollar amount represented roughly 60% of the federal poverty guideline for a family of three.) In a large majority of states (73% or 37 states), eligibility for federal Title IV-E foster care assistance is limited to children removed from homes with countable income that is 50% or less of the 2009 federal poverty guidelines.[32] The total number of children in foster care on the last day of FY2000 was approximately 552,000, and during that fiscal year an estimated 52% of children in foster care received Title IV-E assistance. By comparison, on the last day of FY2008 (the most recent year for which data are available) there were some 463,000 children in foster care and an estimated 43% were eligible for Title IV-E foster care assistance.[33]

While the decline in the Title IV-E caseload pushed the FY2011 request for Title IV-E assistance down, several proposed or recently enacted policy changes required HHS to assume the need for additional Title IV-E foster care funding. These changes limited the effect of the caseload decline on the budget request. For example, the FY2011 budget request includes additional funds sought to provide enhanced federal matching funds as authorized by ARRA for the first three months of the fiscal year, as well as funds to continue this enhanced match (at 6.1 percentage points) for an additional six months as proposed by the President's FY2011 budget. As noted earlier, Congress has acted to extend enhanced federal funding for six months but at a lower rate than requested by the President. In addition, the Fostering Connections to Success and Increasing Adoptions Act of 2008 (P.L. 110-351) phases in (over five years) increased federal support for training private child welfare agency workers and certain other specified individuals. Additionally, beginning with FY2011, that same law will permit states to extend federal Title IV-E foster care assistance to eligible youth who remain in care beyond their 18th birthday, and states that take advantage of this new ability may be expected to have increased Title IV-E foster care claims.[34]

Kinship Guardianship Assistance

HHS is seeking $86 million during the FY2011 appropriations process to reimburse states for eligible guardianship claims made during the year, compared to $56 million provided for FY2010 (P.L. 111-117).[35] The request for increased funding for this Title IV-E component primarily reflects expected growth in the number of children who will be eligible for guardianship assistance as more states implement this relatively new Title IV-E program option. HHS estimates that an average of 8,500 children will receive Title IV-E guardianship assistance, per month, during FY2010 (which was the first year that states could claim this Title IV-E funding) and that this number will grow to 14,300 in FY2011. The requested increase also includes some additional funds needed to provide enhanced federal support under Title IV-E for nine months of the year. This includes the three months of FY2011 for which this enhanced funding is currently authorized by ARRA and six additional months for which this enhanced match would be continued under a legislative proposal included in the President's FY2011 budget. As noted earlier, Congress has acted to extend enhanced federal funding for six months but at a lower rate than requested by the President.

FY2011 will be the second full year of implementation of this Title IV-E program component which was authorized by the Fostering Connections to Success and Increasing Adoptions Act of 2008 (P.L. 110-351) and many states have not yet opted to participate. As of September 21, 2010, 19 states, including the District of Columbia, had submitted Title IV-E plan amendments to enable them to make claims for federal support of guardianship assistance provided on behalf of eligible children.[36] Of those states, nine had final approval of those amendments (Rhode Island, Pennsylvania, Tennessee, Michigan, Montana, Illinois, New Jersey, Oregon, and the District of Columbia) and the remaining 10 (Maine, Missouri, Connecticut, Massachusetts, Washington, Colorado, Nebraska, South Dakota, Maryland, and Texas) had plan amendments that were under review by HHS/ACF or were being revised. [37] Tennessee is the only state to have submitted claims for federal reimbursement of Title IV-E kinship guardianship assistance support in FY2009. The state provided this Title IV-E assistance to 103 children (on an average monthly basis) and claimed federal reimbursement of about $207,000 for that support.[38]

Title IV-B Programs

The President's FY2011 budget proposes the same level of funding provided for FY2010 for each of the child welfare programs and activities authorized under Title IV-B of the Social Security Act. This request for level funding includes two legislative proposals to authorize (for one year) continuation of mandatory funding for certain court improvement, and separately research efforts, authorized under Title IV-B.

Most funding under Title IV-B of the Social Security Act is provided through the Stephanie Tubbs Jones Child Welfare Services program (subpart 1) and the Promoting Safe and Stable Families program (Subpart 2). Under these programs, funds are distributed to all states for child and family services. There are no federal eligibility rules for recipients under these programs. Services may be provided to children and their families in their own homes (e.g., to strengthen or preserve that home and prevent need for removal of children); to the parents of children who are in foster care (e.g., to permit children and their parents to be reunited); to children who are in foster care; to families where the risk of abuse or neglect of children is considered elevated; and to adoptive families (e.g., services to promote adoption and to ensure its success). Under the Court Improvement Program (Section 438 of the Social Security Act), the highest court in each state receives grants to assess and improve the way it handles child welfare related cases, including grants for data collection and training. Section 426 of the Social Security Act authorizes funding for projects related to child welfare training, research, and demonstration. Finally, Section 429 of the Social Security Act requires HHS to fund a longitudinal and nationally representative study of children who are abused or neglected or who are at risk of abuse or neglect.

Stephanie Tubbs Jones Child Welfare Services

The President's FY2011 budget requests $282 million for the Stephanie Tubbs Jones Child Welfare Services Program. This amount is identical to the annual funding appropriated for this program for each of FY2008-FY2010. Funding authorization for this program is described as "discretionary," which means Congress has full authority to decide the funding level for the program in the annual appropriations process. The full annual funding authorization level for this program, $325 million, was established two decades ago (P.L. 101-239, enacted December 1989), but has never been appropriated. However, at its funding highpoint the program did receive close to $295 million in each of FY1 993 and FY1994.[39]

Promoting Safe and Stable Families

The President's FY20 11 budget requests $408 million for the Promoting Safe and Stable Families program. This amount is identical to the annual funding appropriated for the program in each of FY2008-FY2010. While the

Promoting Safe and Stable Families program primarily provides funds to states, territories, and tribes to support services to children and their families, the statute also provides that some program funding must be reserved for (1) improved court handling of child welfare proceedings; (2) research, evaluation, and technical assistance activities related to those services; (3) monthly caseworker visits to children in foster care; and (4) competitive grants to support services that improve outcomes for children affected by parental/caretaker abuse of methamphetamine or another substance.[40]

Under current law, Congress has authorized (through FY2011) both mandatory and discretionary appropriations for the Promoting Safe and Stable Families program. Total program funding authorized for FY2011 (as provided by P.L. 111-242) is $565 million. Of that sum, $365 million is "mandatory," which means each state is statutorily entitled to receive a certain share of that funding, and the remaining $200 million is authorized on a discretionary basis, which means Congress can choose to provide all, some, or none of these authorized dollars. Since the discretionary funding authorization was enacted in 2002 (P.L. 107-133), the appropriation for the program has never reached its full funding authorization level. Funding provided under the discretionary authorization peaked in FY2004 at $100 million, but subsequently declined to $63 million in each of FY2008-FY20 11.

Court Improvement Program

As noted above, a portion of funds provided for the Promoting Safe and Stable Families Program ($12 million in recent years) is reserved each year for formula grants to states' highest courts to assess and improve their handling of child welfare proceedings (Section 438 of the Social Security Act). In addition to these set-aside funds, the Deficit Reduction Act of 2005 (P.L. 109- 171) appropriated a total of $100 million for additional Court Improvement Program grants ($20 million in each of FY2006-FY20 10) that are related to court data collection and training. The President's FY20 11 budget requested a one-year extension of funding for these grants, and as part of the recently enacted Continuing Appropriations Act, FY20 11 (P.L. 111-242), Congress authorized the continuation of these two CIP grants. That law increased mandatory funding by $20 million under the Promoting Safe and Stable Families program (for FY20 11), and directed that this additional funding be set aside to support the court training and data collection CIP grants.[41]

Child Welfare Research, Training, and Demonstration

The President's FY2011 budget seeks $27 million for the research and demonstration activities authorized under Section 426 of the Social Security Act; this is equal to the sum provided for that purpose for FY2010 but is $20 million more than was provided under this section in most recent years.

Section 426 of the Social Security Act provides permanent, discretionary funding authority for HHS to make grants or contracts with a variety of entities for research and demonstration projects related to child welfare activities. From FY1996 through FY2009, this authority was used solely to provide support for child welfare *training* related activities. The President's FY20 10 budget, however, requested a continuation of those training funds as well as a new appropriation of $20 million to support demonstrations of innovative approaches to reduce the number of children who stay in foster care for extended periods of time. [42] Congress matched this request by providing a total of $27 million under the Section 426 funding authority (P.L. 111-117), of which $20 million is expected to be used for the new demonstration program.

On June 8, 2010, HHS, ACF, Administration for Children, Youth, and Families released a funding opportunity announcement for the "Initiative to Reduce Long-Term Foster Care."[43] The initiative is expected to fund five demonstration projects for five years, with annual maximum federal funding of $2.5 million for each successful applicant. Applicants may be state or county governments, tribal governments or organizations, public or private institutions of higher education and nonprofits. They must provide a 10% match (in cash or in-kind) and must develop cooperative agreements with the Children's Bureau to (1) implement intervention strategies to reduce long-term foster stays (i.e., three years or more) for children in foster care and improve child outcomes; and (2) rigorously evaluate these efforts to provide information about effectiveness of the programs, interventions, and practices implemented. Grantees may focus their efforts at a variety of service points (e.g., before children enter foster care, at the point of entry, or after children have been in care for a longer period of time). They may also focus on recruitment of foster homes in communities with high removal rates among other efforts intended to improve family well-being and child welfare practice. HHS will designate an evaluator to conduct site- specific as well as cross-site evaluations. The application deadline was August 9, 2010.[44]

Study of Children Abused or Neglected or at Risk of Abuse or Neglect

The President's FY2011 budget includes a legislative proposal to continue mandatory funding ($6 million) under Section 429 of the Social Security Act for research concerning children who are at risk of abuse or neglect or who have been abused or neglected. Congress provided a full one-year extension of this mandatory funding in P.L. 111-242. This funding will enable HHS to continue to support a second phase of the research study known as the National Survey of Child and Adolescent Well-Being (NSCAW). First authorized as part of the welfare reform legislation that created the Temporary Assistance to Needy Families (TANF) block grant (P.L. 104-193), this research provides nationally representative and longitudinal data on children and families that come into contact with child protective services via an investigation of alleged child abuse or neglect.[45]

Adoption Incentives

The President's FY2011 budget seeks $42 million in discretionary appropriations for the Adoption Incentive program, which is $2.5 million above funding provided for these awards as part of the FY2010 appropriations process. The Senate Appropriations Committee has approved legislation (S. 3686) that would provide the requested $42 million for these program.

Adoption Incentives are authorized under Section 473A of the Social Security Act. That section of the law requires HHS to award bonuses to states that increase adoptions out of foster care. States are permitted to spend this award money to provide any service to children or families, including post-adoption services, that is authorized by the federal child welfare programs (under Title IV-B or Title IV-E of the Social Security Act). States helped finalize record numbers of adoptions out of foster care in both FY2008 and FY2009. And in both years, funding for the Adoption Incentive program has fallen below the total amount states were calculated to have earned for increases in the number and rate of adoptions.

The increased FY2011 funding requested for Adoption Incentives is based on both this recent increase in the number of adoptions out of foster care that have been finalized by states as well as changes in the incentive structure that were adopted by Congress in 2008. Beginning with awards made for adoptions finalized in FY2008, the Fostering Connections to Success and Increasing

Adoption Act of 2008 (P.L. 110-351) doubled the amount of incentive funding that may be earned for increases in adoption of older children (age 9 or above) and for children with special needs (under age 9) while maintaining the prior law incentive for an increase in the overall number of adoptions. Further, it fixed the state-by-state baseline number of adoptions that must be exceeded in order for a state to earn Adoption Incentive awards to the number of adoptions finalized during FY2007. Finally, it added a bonus (provided sufficient funds were appropriated) for states that increase the rate at which children are adopted from foster care.[46]

HHS has interpreted the statute to permit the full award to states for any increases based on the *number* of child adoptions finalized—provided sufficient appropriations are available at the time of the initial award or are made available in a subsequent year. At the same time, it has read the statute to provide that an increase in adoptions linked solely to a change in the adoption *rate* (newly available beginning with adoptions finalized for FY2008) may only be provided if funds are available to make these bonus payments when the initial awards are made.

Recent Adoption Incentive Awards History

For FY2008, states helped finalize the adoptions of close to 54,300 children who were formerly in foster care[47] and HHS awarded Adoption Incentive funds totaling $35.4 million. Of this amount, $33.7 million was distributed to 38 states and the District of Columbia, which covered 100% of award amounts earned for an increase in the *number* of adoptions in those jurisdictions. An additional $1.0 million was provided to 24 states[48] for increases in the *rate* of overall foster child adoption. That amount was a little less than half of the $3.5 million that HHS calculated those states earned for adoption rate increases. Accordingly, each of those states received a little less than one-half (48%) of their calculated rate increase award. Currently, no further Adoption Incentive awards are expected to be made based on adoptions finalized in FY2008.[49]

During FY2009, states helped finalize the adoptions of nearly 55,700 children who were formerly in foster care, a new annual record. [50] Based on those adoptions, HHS has, as of September 2010, awarded Adoption Incentive funds of $38.9 million to 38 states and Puerto Rico. This sum represented all of the funds available in that month to make these Adoption Incentive awards. It equals a little less than 89% of the $43.9 million states were calculated to have earned for increasing the *number* of children adopted from foster care and 0% of the amount ($3.5 million) calculated to have been earned by 30 states for increases in the rate of adoption. Provided additional appropriations are made available for FY2009 awards, and assuming past practice is followed, HHS would be expected to distribute the additional award amounts (circa $5 million) linked to increases in the number of adoptions from foster care. However, it would not be expected to provide any additional funds to the 30 states that met the criteria for increased *rates* of adoptions from foster care during FY2009.[51]

Child Abuse Prevention and Treatment Act

The President's FY20 11 budget requests $107 million in funding for the three appropriation accounts funded under the Child Abuse Prevention and Treatment Act (CAPTA), which is $10 million more than FY20 10 funding provided for them. This additional funding is sought by the Administration to establish a new competitive grant program. (See "Proposed Grants Related to Prevention of Child Abuse and Neglect," above.) The Senate Appropriations Committee has approved legislation (S. 3686) that would provide just over $105 million for CAPTA, including the $10 million in new competitive grant funding sought by the Administration.

Funding authority for CAPTA expired with FY2008, however, Congress has continued to provide funding for the program. (The CAPTA Reauthorization Act of 2010, S. 3817, was introduced in the Senate on September 22, 2010, but as of the October 2010 recess had not been acted on.) CAPTA authorizes funding for (1) formula grants to states to help support their child protective services systems, referred to as "child abuse state grants" by appropriators; (2) competitive grants or contracts to support research and demonstration projects related to prevention and treatment of child abuse and neglect, or for other, related activities, referred to as "child abuse discretionary activities"; and (3) formula grants distributed to all states to support community-based activities and services to prevent child abuse and neglect, referred to as "community-based child abuse prevention" by appropriators. (For more information about CAPTA, see CRS Report R40899, *The Child Abuse Prevention and Treatment Act (CAPTA): Background, Programs, and Funding*.)

Table 2. Recent and Proposed Federal Funding Dedicated to Child Welfare ($ in millions; NA = not authorized; amounts shown in italics are funds that have been provided in acts other than major appropriations bills, in whole or in part)

	Final Funding			FY20 1 1 Proposed Funding	
	FY2008	**FY2009**	**FY20 10**	**President's Budget**	**Senate Approp. Cmte.[a]**
Table TOTAL	**$7,858**	**$8,257**	**$8,432**	**$8,512**	**$8,254**
TITLE IV-B, SUBPART I of the Social Security Act					
Stephanie Tubbs Jones Child Welfare Services: Formula grants to states, territories, and tribes to improve child welfare services.	282	282	282	282	282
Child Welfare Training, Research, and Demonstration: Competitive grants to nonprofits or universities for child welfare related research or demonstration and for workforce training.	7	7	27	27	27
Family Connection Grants: Competitive grants to eligible public or nonprofit entities to support kinship navigator programs, special family finding efforts, family group decision-making meetings, and/or residential family treatment programs.[b]	NA	*15*	*15*	*15*	*15*
National Survey of Child and Adolescent Well-Being (NSCAW): Competitive grant to support longitudinal study of children at risk of, or exposed to, child abuse or neglect.[c]	*6*	*6*	*6*	*6*	*0*
TITLE IV-B, SUBPART 2 of the Social Security Act					

Table 2. (Continued)

	Final Funding			FY20 1 1 Proposed Funding	
	FY2008	**FY2009**	**FY20 10**	**President's Budget**	**Senate Approp. Cmte.**[a]
Promoting Safe and Stable Families (PSSF) (subtotal)	**408**	**408**	**408**	**408**	**408**
PSSF: Formula grants to states, territories, and tribes for family preservation, support, time-limited reunification, and adoption promotion and support services. (Includes fund reserved for HHS to conduct program-related research, evaluations, and technical assistance in each year.)	356	356	356	356	356
***PSSF- Monthly Caseworker Visits with Foster Children**:* Formula grants to states and territories to support quality, monthly caseworker visits with children in foster care.d	5	10	20	20	20
***PSSF -Child Welfare and Substance Abuse**:* Competitive grants to regional partnerships to improve outcomes of children affected by parent or caretaker abuse of methamphetamine (or other substances).[d]	35	30	20	20	20
Court Improvement Program: Formula grants to states' highest courts to improve handling of child welfare proceedings. (Funding shown includes set-aside from PSSF subtotal and separate $20 million in pre-appropriated funds, not included in PSSF subtotal.)[e]	*32*	*32*	*32*	*32*	*12*

Table 2. (Continued)

	Final Funding			FY20 1 1 Proposed Funding	
	FY2008	FY2009	FY20 10	President's Budget	Senate Approp. Cmte.[a]
TITLE IV-E of the Social Security Act					
Foster Care: Open-ended reimbursement of eligible state claims for children in foster care and for related data collection, administrative, and training costs.[f]	4,581	4,660[g]	4,681	4,645	4,539[h]
Adoption Assistance: Open-ended reimbursement of eligible state claims for subsidies to special needs adoptees and related administrative and training costs.[f]	2,156	2,371[g]	2,501[g]	2,585	2,459
Kinship Guardianship Assistance: Open-ended reimbursement of eligible state claims for subsidies to eligible children who leave foster care for legal guardianship with a relative and for related administrative and training costs.[f]	NA	14	56[g]	83	78
Technical Assistance and Tribal Implementation: Competitive grants for technical assistance to tribes and states (to improve services to and outcomes for the Indian children they serve) and for implementation funds (to tribes preparing to submit a Title IV-E plan to claim direct federal support).[i]	NA	*3*	*3*	*3*	*3*
Adoption Incentives: Bonus funds to states that increase foster child adoptions.	4.3	36.5	39.5	42.0	42.0

Table 2. (Continued)

	Final Funding		FY20 1 1 Proposed Funding		
	FY2008	**FY2009**	**FY20 10**	**President's Budget**	**Senate Approp. Cmte.[a]**
CHAFEE FOSTER CARE INDEPENDENCE PROGRAM					
CFCIP (subtotal)	**185**	**185**	**185**	**185**	**185**
***Basic Program*: Formula grants to states for provision of independent living services to foster youth who have, or are expected to, "age out" of care.**	140	140	140	140	140
***Education and Training Vouchers*: Formula grants to states to provide vouchers for education and training to foster youth who age out of care.**	45.4	45.4	45.4	45.4	45.4
CHILD ABUSE PREVENTION AND TREATMENT ACT					
CAPTA (subtotal)	**105**	**110**	**97**	**107**	**106**
***Basic State Grants:* Formula grants to states and territories to improve their child protection services.**	26.5	26.5	26.5	26.5	26.5
***Discretionary Activities*: Competitive grants for demonstration, research, or other activities to prevent or treat child maltreatment. (FY2008 and FY2009 amount includes funds for home visiting initiative. FY20 11 request seeks new grant initiative.)**	37.1	41.8	29.0	39.0	37.3

Table 2. (Continued)

	Final Funding			FY20 1 1 Proposed Funding	
	FY2008	**FY2009**	**FY20 10**	**President's Budget**	**Senate Approp. Cmte.**[a]
***Community-Based Grants for Child Abuse Prevention*: Formula grants to lead entity in each state and territory to support community-based programs to prevent child abuse and neglect.**[j]	41.7	41.7	41.7	41.7	41.7
CHILDREN'S HEALTH ACT					
Adoption Awareness (subtotal)	**12.5**	**13.0**	**13.0**	**0k**	**0k**
Infant Adoption Awareness: Competitive grants to train staff in nonprofit health centers about adoption counseling.	9.6	10.1	10.1	0k	0k
Special Needs Adoption Awareness: Competitive grants for a public campaign about adoption of children with special needs.	2.9	2.9	2.9	0k	0k
OTHER PROGRAMS					
***Adoption Opportunities*:** Competitive grants to eliminate barriers to adoptions—especially special needs adoptions.	26.4	26.4	26.4	39.3[k]	39.3[k]
***Abandoned Infants Assistance*:** Competitive grants to prevent abandonment of infants exposed to HIV/AIDS or drugs and for services and programs to address needs of abandoned children.	11.6	11.6	11.6	11.6	11.6

Table 2. (Continued)

	Final Funding			FY20 1 1 Proposed Funding	
	FY2008	FY2009	FY20 10	President's Budget	Senate Approp. Cmte.[a]
Children's Justice Act Grants: Formula grant to states and tribes to improve the handling of child abuse and neglect cases.[1]	20	20	*20*	*20*	*20*
VICTIMS OF CHILD ABUSE ACT					
***Children's Advocacy Centers*:** Competitive grants for services to child victims of abuse (and non-offending family members), to coordinate child abuse investigations in ways that reduce their trauma, and for related training and technical assistance.	16.9	20.0	22.5	20.0	22.5
***Court Appointed Special Advocates*:** Competitive grants to support court advocates for child victims of abuse and neglect.	13.2	15.0	15.0	10.0	14.2
Training for Judicial Practitioners and Personnel: Competitive grant to improve handling of child abuse and neglect cases.	2.4	2.5	2.5	2.5	2.5

Source: Prepared by the Congressional Research Service (CRS).

a. This column includes FY20 1 1 recommendations approved by the Senate Appropriations Committee as part of S. 3686 (S.Rept. 111-243) and S. 3636 (S.Rept. 111-229). Certain child welfare accounts received "pre- appropriated" funds, which means their appropriations were included in legislation enacted separately from the appropriations process. Funding that has already been appropriated for these accounts is shown in this column in italics.

b. Funds for these grants ($15 million for each of FY2009-FY20 13) were appropriated as part of the Fostering Connections to Success and Increasing Adoptions Act of 2008 (P.L. 110-351). They are therefore assumed to be part of the President's FY20 11 budget and are not shown in the annual appropriations bills.

c. Funds for this survey ($6 million for each of FY2006-FY20 10) were appropriated as part of the Deficit Reduction Act of 2005 (P.L. 109-171). Therefore, they did not appear in annual appropriations bills. For FY20 11, and as requested by the President, Congress pre-appropriated $6 million for this research as part of P.L. 111-242 (enacted September 30, 2010).

d. Section 436(b) (as amended by P.L. 109-288) stipulates that for FY2007-FY20 11, out of mandatory funds authorized for appropriation under the PSSF program, $40 million is to be divided (as specified) for two targeted purposes: monthly caseworker visits to children in foster care and grants to improve child welfare outcomes of children affected by a caretaker's abuse of methamphetamine or another substance.

e. The funding for Court Improvement includes $20 million that was appropriated annually (for each of FY2006-FY2010) by the Deficit Reduction Act of 2005 (P.L. 109-171). Therefore, it did not appear in annual appropriations bills. For FY20 11, and as requested by the President, Congress authorized mandatory funding of $20 million for this research as part of P.L. 111-242 (enacted September 30, 2010).

f. Each year, the appropriation for this Title IV-E account includes an advance amount to permit HHS to make payments for the first quarter of the next year. For purposes of annual comparison, the full amount appropriated (including the advance) is shown as part of funding made available each year.

g. The final funding amount shown is different from previous versions of this report because HHS has indicated it has (or will) use indefinite budget authority (included in the annual appropriations bills).

h. This appropriation amount does not include funds authorized by P.L. 111-226, which permits states to receive an enhanced FMAP in fiscal quarters 2 and 3 (of 3.2 percentage points and 1.2 percentage points, respectively). HHS estimates this will increase budget authority for the overall Title IV-E program by $75 million in FY20 11. However, this is less than the $237 million the President's budget requested to extend the enhanced FMAP at 6.2 percentage points for both of those quarters.

i. Funds for these grants ($3 million for FY2009 and every succeeding fiscal year) were appropriated as part of the Fostering Connections to Success and Increasing Adoptions Act of 2008 (P.L. 110-351). They are therefore assumed to be part of the President's FY20 1 1 budget and are not shown in the annual appropriations bills.

j. This program also authorizes a 1% set-aside of appropriated funds for grants to tribes and migrant programs.

k. The President's FY20 11 budget seeks to redirect all funding for Adoption Awareness to the Adoption Opportunities program. The Senate Appropriations Committee recommends following this request.

l. Program authority for these grants is included in CAPTA but annual funding is set aside from the Crime Victims Fund (as provided by the Victims of Crime Act, P.L. 98-473, as amended). Therefore, funds are not provided for them from the general treasury and are not shown in an individual appropriations account.

Victims of Child Abuse Act

The Victims of Child Abuse Act authorizes funding for Children's Advocacy Centers, Court Appointed Special Advocates (CASA), and Training for Judges and Judicial Practitioners. The President's FY20 11 budget seeks $10 million for CASA, as compared to the $15 million it received in FY2009 and FY20 10. It seeks $2.5 million for training for judicial judges and practitioners, which is identical to funding provided for this purpose in each of FY2009 and FY20 11. It also seeks $20 million for Children's Advocacy Centers, including related training and technical assistance, which is less than the $22.5 million provided for them in FY2010 but equal to their funding in FY2009.

The Senate Appropriations Committee recommends funding for CASA of $14.2 million; funding for Training of Judges and Judicial Practitioners of $2.5 million; and funding for the Children's Advocacy Centers, including related training and technical assistance, of $22.5 million (S.Rept. 111-229).

Funding authorization for Children's Advocacy Centers and training for judges and judicial practitioners expired with FY2005 but the programs have continued to receive annual funding. Funding authorization for CASA was extended through FY2011 as part of the Violence Against Women and Department of Justice Reauthorization Act of 2005 (P.L. 109-1 62).[52]

FUNDING FOR CHILD WELFARE BY PROGRAM

Table 2 lists the federal funding streams dedicated to child welfare purposes that were included in this analysis, briefly describes their purposes, and shows their recent and proposed funding levels.

End Notes

[1] See discussion of child welfare provisions in CRS Report R40211, *Human Services Provisions of the American Recovery and Reinvestment Act*, by Gene Falk et al.

[2] Enhanced federal support is made available through an increase in the Federal Medical Assistance Percentage, known as the FMAP. The FMAP is also used to determine the amount of federal support states receive for certain Medicaid costs. For more information, see CRS Report RL32950, *Medicaid: The Federal Medical Assistance Percentage (FMAP).*

[3] Informal CRS communication with staff at HHS, ACF, Office of Legislative Affairs and Budget.

[4] For more information, see discussion of changes made to the Court Improvement Program by P.L. 109-171 in CRS Report RL33350, *Child Welfare: The Court Improvement Program*, by Emilie Stoltzfus.

[5] For more information on funding for this research, first authorized by P.L. 104-193, and some findings, see *Green Book 2008*, Child Welfare, p. 11-106 and 11-151 through 11-155. Available on the House Ways and Means Committee website at http://waysandmeans.house.gov/media

[6] U.S. Department of Health and Human Services, Administration for Children and Families, *Justification of Estimates for Appropriations Committees, FY2011*, (hereafter cited as HHS, ACF, FY201 1 Budget Justifications), p. 115.

[7] S.Rept. 111-243, to accompany S. 3686, p. 154.

[8] The program was authorized to receive funding of $40 million for FY2004 and "such sums as may be necessary" for each of FY2005-FY2008.

[9] Under the Infant Adoption Awareness component, HHS is authorized to make competitive grants to adoption organizations to train staff at eligible public and private nonprofit health centers on informing pregnant women about adoption and, as requested, on making referrals to adoption agencies on an equal basis with all other courses of action. Funds appropriated for this purpose have been roughly $9 million or $10 million annually in each of FY2001-FY2010. Most recently, HHS awarded five-year Infant Adoption Awareness grants (scheduled to end with FY20 10) to six organizations for projects considered national in scope as well as regional or local projects.

[10] Under the Special Needs Adoption Awareness component, HHS is authorized to make grants to nonprofit groups to plan, develop, and carry out a national campaign informing the public about the adoption of children with special needs. Funding available for this component of the Adoption Awareness program has been roughly $3 million in each of FY2001-FY2010 and has primarily supported development of public service announcements.

[11] The programs were authorized to receive "such sums as may be necessary" for each of FY2001-FY2005.

[12] HHS, ACF, FY20 11 Budget Justifications, p. 133.

[13] S.Rept. 111-243, to accompany S. 3686, pp. 155-156.

[14] Ibid, p. 156.

[15] S.Rept. 111-229, to accompany S. 3636, p. 96.

[16] U.S. Department of Justice, Office of Justice Programs, *FY2011 Performance Budget*, p. 79.

[17] Separately, P.L. 109-162 authorized training and technical assistance funds of $7.5 million (for each of FY2006- FY20 10) related to purposes of Children's Advocacy Centers. However, that law referenced but did not amend the Victims of Child Abuse Act funding authorization for this program.

[18] U.S. Department of Justice, Office of Justice Programs, *FY2011 Performance Budget,* p. 115.

[19] This funding share counts the $20 million provided to states and tribes via the Children's Justice Act grants, which are provided as a set-aside from the Crime Victims Fund (rather than out of the general treasury).

[20] For more information, see CRS Report R4021 8, *Youth Transitioning from Foster Care: Issues for Congress*, by Adrienne L. Fernandes-Alcantara.

[21] Funding for this initiative was initially requested by the Bush Administration in the FY2008 budget request. On September 30, 2008, HHS awarded the initial home visitation grants to 17 grantees in 15 states. These grantees intended to help implement or enhance and study a variety of home visiting models (alone or in combination), including the Nurse Family Partnership, Healthy Families America, Parents as Teachers, Safe Care, and others. In addition, HHS awarded funds to Mathematica Policy Research, Inc., and Chapin Hall Center for Children to conduct a cross-site evaluation of the grantees' programs, including (1) an implementation study, (2) a fidelity and outcomes study, and (3) a cost study. Mathematica and Chapin Hall must also establish and coordinate a peer learning network to facilitate information sharing and will provide evaluation technical assistance to grantees

and their local evaluators through this network. See "Supporting Evidence-Based Home Visiting to Prevent Child Maltreatment," at http://www.acf.hhs.gov/programs/cb/programs_fund/discretionary/visitation/ebhv_project

[22] H.Rept. 111-366, p. 1038. Prior to this conference decision, the House had approved legislation that would have provided $15 million to fund the initiative's third year (H.R. 3293 as passed in July 2009) and the Senate Appropriations Committee had approved third-year funding of $13.5 million (S.Rept. 111-66, reported August 2009).

[23] As part of the FY2010 budget request, the Obama Administration requested mandatory funding ($1.5 billion over five years) for a new state grant program to support home visiting programs for low-income mothers and pregnant women. Before Congress enacted the new home visiting program as part of the health care reform (P.L. 111-148), both the House (H.R. 3962, as passed November 6, 2008), and the Senate (H.R. 3590, as passed December 24, 2008) included funding to support a new program of grants to states for evidence-based early childhood home visitation. For more information, see CRS Report R40705, *Home Visitation for Families with Young Children*, by Emilie Stoltzfus and Karen E. Lynch.

[24] See funding opportunity for the new home visiting program (link available at http://www.hrsa.gov/about/news/ pressreleases/100610.html) and U.S. Department of Health and Human Services, Health Resources Administration and Administration for Children and Families, "Maternal, Infant, and Early Childhood Home Visiting Program," June 17, 2010 (Powerpoint slides) available at http://www.cademedia.com/archives/mchb/director/20100617/ 201006 17_MCHB_Director_HomeVisitingProgram.pdf.

[25] For each fiscal year, the definite budget authority requested by HHS includes a certain amount expected to be necessary to make timely payments to states for Title IV-E claims during the first quarter of the following fiscal year. Because funding is requested this way each year, for comparability the total budget authority sought in a given year (regardless of the year for which it is sought) is discussed as the budget request for the given year (e.g., FY20 11 request).

[26] Beginning with FY2003, in its annual appropriation bills Congress has provided additional funding authority of "such sums as may be necessary" to allow HHS to reimburse states for any eligible amounts in the last quarter of the fiscal year that are *above* the definite amount appropriated for that fiscal year.

[27] This FY20 10 amount reflects funds provided under the "indefinite" budget authority included for the Title IV-E program in the appropriations process. The definite Title IV-E adoption assistance amount included in P.L. 111-117, as described in an earlier version of this report, was $2.462 billion.

[28] HHS, ACF, *FY2011 Budget Justifications*, pp. 327-328 and 330, and unpublished Title IV-E expenditure claim data for FY2009 provided to CRS by ACF.

[29] FY2010 was the first year in which the provisions included in P.L. 110-351 to phase in new federal eligibility for Title IV-E adoption assistance were in place. During FY20 10, the phase-in applies principally to children adopted at age 16 or 17 during that same fiscal year. During FY20 11, it will apply, principally, to children adopted at age 14 or older. Children who are siblings of youth meeting these age eligibility criteria and who are to be placed in the same adoptive home with their siblings may also be eligible without regard to the income or resource test. Finally, any otherwise eligible child who is adopted after spending 60 continuous months in foster care is also eligible without regard to income or resource test. Also, beginning with FY20 11 states will have the option to extend (until age 21) federal adoption assistance to otherwise eligible youth who were adopted after their 16th birthday. Under current law, this federal assistance generally ends at age 18.

[30] HHS, ACF, *FY2011 Budget Justifications*, p. 330.

[31] The prior law cash welfare program was known as Aid to Families with Dependent Children (AFDC). It was repealed by Congress in 1996 (P.L. 104-193) and replaced by the Temporary Assistance for Needy Families (TANF) block grant.

[32] CRS calculations based on unpublished 1996 need standard data (for a family of three) received from HHS compared to the federal poverty guidelines. "States" as discussed here include the District of Columbia (i.e., total of 51 states). Many states paid monthly benefits (referred to as "payment standards") that were less than a state's need standard. States determined their own need standard, as required by federal law, and this standard represented the maximum amount of countable income a family could have and be eligible for AFDC. Federal law additionally established that no family could be eligible for AFDC if it had *gross* income above 185% of the state's need standard. The median (annualized) *gross* income limitation for a family of three is about $15,300, or 83%, of the 2009 federal poverty guidelines for a family of three.

[33] Their are additional reasons that children may not be eligible for Title IV-E assistance, including, for example, the child's placement in a unlicensed foster family home or care facility. Further, the share of children eligible for Title IV- E foster care assistance varies greatly by state and it can be estimated in more than one way. For a discussion of Title IV-E eligibility criteria and various estimates of the federal Title IV-E foster care coverage rate over time, see *Green Book 2008*, Child Welfare, pp. 11-52 through 11-57, available on the website of the House Ways and Means Committee at http://waysandmeans.house.gov/media

[34] HHS, ACF, *FY2011 Budget Justifications*, pp. 327 and 330. See also CRS Report RL34704, *Child Welfare: The Fostering Connections to Success and Increasing Adoptions Act of 2008*, by Emilie Stoltzfus.

[35] This FY2010 amount reflects funds provided under the "indefinite" budget authority included for the Title IV-E program in the appropriations process. The definite Title IV-E kinship guardianship assistance amount included in P.L. 111-117, as described in an earlier version of this report, was $49 million.

[36] Among other requirements, children eligible for Title IV-E guardianship assistance must leave foster care for placement in a legal guardianship with a relative and they must have been eligible for Title IV-E foster care maintenance payments while living with that relative for at least six consecutive months. In revised program guidance issued February 18, 2010, HHS/ACF notes that children eligible for this Title IV-E assistance may include children who left foster care for guardianship prior to enactment of P.L. 110-351, provided that child meets all the other eligibility requirements for the payments. See program instruction ACYF-CB-PI-10-01, issued by HHS, ACF, available at http://www.acf.hhs.gov/programs/cb/laws

[37] Based on CRS communication with ACF.

[38] This represented about 70.4% of Tennessee kinship guardianship assistance expenditures for Title IV-E eligible children. (Total expenditures were just under $294,000.)

[39] For more information about this program and its most recent reauthorization see CRS Report RL33354, The Promoting Safe and Stable Families Program: Reauthorization in the 109th Congress, by Emilie Stoltzfus.

[40] Ibid.

[41] For more information, see CRS Report RL33350, *Child Welfare: The Court Improvement Program, by Emilie Stoltzfus*; and CRS Report RL33354, *The Promoting Safe and Stable Families Program: Reauthorization in the 109th Congress*, by Emilie Stoltzfus.

[42] HHS, ACF, *FY2010 Justification of Estimates for Appropriations Committees*, pp. 137-138.

[43] The funding announcement is available at http://www.acf.hhs.gov/grants/

[44] Ibid.

[45] For more information on the survey and for a list of research briefs from the NSCAW study see http://www.acf.hhs.gov/programs/opre/abuse

[46] For more information on changes in the incentive structure made by P.L. 110-351, see CRS Report RL34704, *Child Welfare: The Fostering Connections to Success and Increasing Adoptions Act of 2008*, by Emilie Stoltzfus.

[47] The number of adoptions out of foster care is typically slightly lower than the number of all adoptions with some public child welfare agency involvement because a small number of

those adoptions concerned children who were not previously in foster care. See HHS, ACF, ACYF, Children's Bureau, *The AFCARS Report* # 16 (October 2009).

48 With the exception of one state (Montana), all states that earned an incentive for an increase in adoption rate also earned an incentive based on an increase in adoption rate.

49 A link to states receiving FY2008 awards is included in the HHS press release announcing these awards at http://www.hhs.gov/news/press/2009pres/09/20090914a.html. Final award amounts given at the link are correct for all but two states. HHS adjusted the payout amounts to Maine (actual award $73,280) and Tennessee (actual award $554,400) after identifying an initial error in calculation of those state's award amounts. Based on CRS communication with staff at HHS, ACF, ACYF, Children's Bureau.

50 See HHS, ACF, ACYF, Children's Bureau, *The AFCARS Report* # 17.

51 Based on CRS communication with staff at HHS, ACF, ACYF, Children's Bureau. Twenty-seven of the 30 jurisdictions that met the criteria for an adoption rate increase award also earned an incentive based on an increase in adoption rate. (The three states that met the rate increase award criteria only were CO, MA, NJ.) For FY2009 awards by state see http://www.acf.hhs.gov/news/press/2010/fy10_adoption_incentive_awards.htm.

52 See CRS Report RL34252, *Child Welfare: Federal Policy Changes Enacted in the 109th Congress*, by Emilie Stoltzfus.

CHAPTER SOURCES

Chapter 1 - This is an edited, reformatted and augmented edition of a Congressional Research Service publication, RL34704, dated October 9, 2008.

Chapter 2 - This is an edited, reformatted and augmented edition of a Congressional Research Service publication, RL33855, dated January 28, 2010.

Chapter 3 - This is an edited, reformatted and augmented edition of a Congressional Research Service publication, RL34121, dated October 7, 2010.

INDEX

D

E

F

M

N

O

P

Q

R

U

V

W